BIRN...ES

D0395618

Walt Disney World
DINING GUIDE

Wendy Lefkon
EDITORIAL DIRECTOR

Jill Safro
EDITOR

THE
OFFICIAL
GUIDE

Jessica Ward
CONTRIBUTING EDITOR

Lois Spritzer and Pam Brandon
CONTRIBUTING WRITERS

Alexandra Mayes Birnbaum
CONSULTING EDITOR

A COMPLETE INSIDER'S GUIDE TO DINING DISNEY STYLE

DISNEP EDITIONS

NEW YORK • LOS ANGELES

For Steve Birnbaum, who merely made all of this possible.

A Word from the Editor

It has been said (and sung) that "it's a small world after all." It is not. In fact, Disney's world is so vast and has dining places so plentiful (there are hundreds of them) that picking the right spot to satisfy your group's diverse tastes can be a daunting experience.

It doesn't have to be. We assure you that whatever your palate prefers—simple or sublime, fast food or fine dining—it's being served up somewhere at Walt Disney World. Of course, finding (and reserving) the meal of your dreams can be a challenge. That's where this book comes in. If you're in search of a light snack or a filling lunch, a character breakfast or a champagne brunch—you'll find it described within these pages. You'll also discover rousing dinner shows, theme park favorites, quiet gems off the beaten path, and much more.

Given the popularity of WDW eateries, booking a table in advance is nearly as important as selecting a venue. Our "WDW reservations" explanation will help you do it.

Don't forget, you also need to be thinking about what you want to do later in the evening. Please, take your time, and when you're ready to strategize after-dinner entertainment, just flip to our Pubs and Lounges chapter. It delivers the scoop on Downtown Disney and the BoardWalk entertainment zones, as well as compelling spots in the parks and resorts.

Rest assured, a lot of time and calories have gone into the creation of the dining guide you're holding. This is not merely an alphabetical restaurant listing—there are telephone books for that. Our hardy band of editorial gourmands has visited each and every establishment and sampled the fare. If we love a place, you'll know. If we agree that an eatery isn't worth a rave, it won't get one. But our opinions are just that, opinions. The truth is, one reader may see a giant turkey leg as a meal fit for a queen, while the same snack leaves another feeling decidedly less regal. We understand that. Our goal is to provide all readers with the information necessary to ensure a successful Disney dining experience.

Chapters in this book are organized by Walt Disney World's parks and resort hotels, with one section focused on eateries within the Downtown Disney entertainment district, another devoted to dinner shows, and one focused on pubs and lounges. We've also included two bonus chapters: The first describes the Disney Dining Plan, and the second reveals some of the most revered and requested recipes in WDW history.

Dining establishments are noted for location, food quality and variety, and ambience. Within each entry there is a price rating and a listing of the meals served. Signature dishes may be listed, but menus (and chefs) do change, so if the braised lamb shank is *the* reason you're headed for a certain restaurant, it's best to call ahead.

If a seven-course gourmet meal is a crucial part of your vacation happiness, you're in luck. If you'd rather enjoy breakfast with Mickey Mouse or have lunch in a castle, you won't be disappointed. It's also possible to dine on couscous in Morocco, stroll to Germany for a knockwurst, to France for quiche, or to the United Kingdom for bangers and mash with a side of mushy peas (don't scoff—it's delicious). In other words, the gastronomic opportunities at Walt Disney World are bountiful, with nearly 6,000 different dishes on its collective menu. From appetizer to dessert, and even a nightcap, we hope this fills the bill.

Bon appétit!

— Jill Safro, Editor

HELPING HANDS

This book was made possible thanks to a tireless team of dedicated diners and behind-the-scenes support. Special, heartfelt thanks go to Heather Reed Guay and to Karen McClintock, who have done so much to ensure the accuracy of *Birnbaum's Official Walt Disney World Dining Guide*.

Kudos to Diane Hodges, copy editor extraordinaire. Thanks also to Jennifer Eastwood, Marybeth Tregarthen, Clark Wakabayashi, Warren Meislin, and Michelle Olveira for their editorial support and production panache. Any list of acknowledgments would be incomplete without mentioning our founding editor, Steve Birnbaum, who continues to be an inspiration for us all, as well as Alexandra Mayes Birnbaum, who is a guiding light and careful reader of every word.

RESERVATION TRACKER

After placing a call to 407-WDW-DINE
(939-3463) to book meals for your
upcoming vacation, jot the details and
confirmation numbers on this page!

_____

_____

_____

_____

_____

_____

_____

_____

_____

_____

_____

_____

_____

_____

Table of Contents

A GUIDE TO THIS GUIDE

This book is a comprehensive guide, with details about each and every eatery on Walt Disney World property. Rather than present you with a book of epic proportions, we've labored to keep the project pocket-sized by combining concise descriptions with handy symbols. Each restaurant entry is preceded by a symbol that indicates whether the establishment is a fast-food spot or a table-service restaurant. We've also indicated whether or not said restaurant is a participant in the Disney Dining Plan (refer to page 13 for details). Here's a rundown of the symbols:

🏃	= Fast Food (aka quick service)
🍴	= Table Service
🐭	= Disney Dining Plan participant
B	= Breakfast
L	= Lunch
D	= Dinner
S	= Snack
$	= Under $15
$$	= $15–$36
$$$	= $36–$60
$$$$	= $60 and up

Prices are estimates based on an average adult dinner consisting of a soft drink, entrée, and either one appetizer, side order, or dessert *before* tax and tip. (Breakfast and lunch generally cost less.)

8

How to Book a WDW Table

The guide you are holding will help you select an ideal locale in which to enjoy every Walt Disney World meal. Picking the perfect place, however, is merely step one in the Disney dining experience. We cannot overemphasize the importance of the follow-up step: *booking* it—well in advance. For an explanation of WDW's unique reservations system, turn the page.

WALT DISNEY WORLD RESERVATIONS

Walt Disney World has reservations about reservations. It seems the traditional system inevitably led to delays, thanks to no-shows and latecomers. As a means of expediting matters, Disney modified the process. Essentially, this means that you arrange to receive priority treatment when it comes to being seated at an agreed-upon time. Here's how it works: Call to request a time at a table-service eatery; arrive about 10 to 15 minutes before the assigned time and check in; receive the next available table that can accommodate your party. (There may be a wait involved.)

If an eatery accepts reservations, make them. Times can be secured up to 180 days ahead; 407-WDW-DINE (939-3463) or *http://disneyworld.disney.go.com/dining/*. Hours are 7 A.M. to 10 P.M. Some restaurants will accommodate walk-ins who are willing to wait—just don't arrive starving!

Some WDW resorts have a phone in the lobby area that provides direct contact with the "Dine Line." Simply touch 55. From theme park pay phones, touch *88 (also toll-free). Otherwise, call 407-WDW-DINE.

HOT TIP

Dining prices for "kids" cover guests ages 3 through 9. Most WDW table-service eateries have special menus just for little ones. Fast-food spots offer kid-friendly items, too. Looking for nutritious choices for your tots? Check the menu for this special Mickey Check symbol: ✔

For same-day arrangements in the Magic
Kingdom, go to City Hall; in Epcot, head
to Guest Relations; in Disney's Hollywood
Studios, go to the corner of Hollywood and
Sunset; in Animal Kingdom, ask at Guest
Relations. Bookings can be made at Down-
town Disney Guest Relations. Of course, plans
may be made at some restaurants themselves.

Keep in mind that a WDW restaurant
reservation is not a traditional reservation. You
may have to wait a while when you arrive at
your assigned time. Rest assured, your party
will be given the first table that opens up.

WHAT DO YOU THINK?

No contribution is of greater value to us
in preparing the next edition of this book
than your comments on what we have
written and on your own Walt Disney
World dining experiences. Please share
your insights with us by writing to:

Jill Safro, Editor
Birnbaum's Walt Disney World Dining Guide 2014
Disney Editions
1133 Sixth Avenue, 33rd Floor
New York, NY 10036

Note that WDW dinner shows (page 113) must be booked in advance. The Hoop-Dee-Doo Musical Revue, the Spirit of Aloha dinner show, and Mickey's Backyard Barbecue accept requests up to 180 days in advance.

Finally, the Disney dining scene is ever-evolving and procedures tend to change from time to time, so we advise calling 407-WDW-DINE (939-3463) to confirm current reservation policies.

NO RESERVATIONS? GOOD LUCK!

Disney's reservations system may allow for walk-ins (who are willing to wait). That said, the popularity of the Disney Dining Plan has made spontaneity something of a challenge. If you get caught without reservations during peak dining hours, consider eating earlier or later than the masses usually do. Here are a few of our favorite table-service places to pop into without an advance reservation (though there is usually a wait involved):

- Big River Grille & Brewing Works (BoardWalk)
- ESPN Club (BoardWalk)
- Hollywood Brown Derby (Disney's Hollywood Studios)
- House of Blues (Downtown Disney, West Side; 407-934-BLUE)
- Il Mulino New York Trattoria (Swan)
- Paradiso 37 (Downtown Disney, between Marketplace and West Side)
- Portobello (Downtown Disney, Marketplace)
- Raglan Road (Downtown Disney, between Marketplace and West Side)
- Todd English's bluezoo (Dolphin)

Disney Dining Plan

To some, it may sound too good to be true: enjoy the convenience of pre-paid meals and stretch your vacation dollar by up to 20–30 percent in the process. But the Disney Dining Plan is just that—a package "add-on" that lets guests redeem meal credits at more than 100 on-property eateries and, by doing so, actually save a few bucks. The plan is flexible, too. Feeling famished? Have an extra snack or a whole meal today and skip one tomorrow. Want to be waited on hand and foot all day? Throw caution to the wind and cash in three table-service meals. Of course, that means you'll have an abundance of quick-service experiences in your future, but who cares? You're on vacation. Do what makes you happy. To learn more about the Disney Dining Plan, turn the page.

The Dining Plan is available to any guest staying at any resort that's owned and operated by Walt Disney World. (That means all resorts on WDW property, with the exception of the Swan, Dolphin, Buena Vista Palace, Best Western Lake Buena Vista, Doubletree Guest Suites, Wyndham, Hilton, Holiday Inn, and B in the WDW Resort.) The plan, which starts at about $40 a day for adults, *must be purchased at the same time the resort is booked.* Together, the room and the Dining Plan are known as the Magic Your Way Plus Dining package. Here's what's included in the basic Dining Plan (there are also Deluxe, Quick Service, Premium, and Platinum packages):

- One "Table Service" meal (includes buffets) per person, per night of the package stay.
- One "Quick Service" meal per person, per night of the package.
- One snack per person, per night of stay.

In other words, if you are booked for 6 nights at, say, the Polynesian or any other Disney-owned-and-operated resort, you are entitled to 6 table-service meals, 6 quick-service meals, and 6 snacks during your stay.

One Table Service Meal includes an entrée, dessert (except at breakfast), and a non-alcoholic beverage, or one full buffet plus soft drink. One non-alcoholic specialty beverage may be substituted for dessert.

HOT TIP

Just because your meals are pre-paid, it doesn't mean they're pre-booked! Make reservations for table-service restaurants by calling 407-WDW-DINE (939-3463).

HOT TIP

Dining Plan participants ages 3–9 are required to order from the kids' menu when one is available.

One Quick Service Meal includes an entrée, dessert (dessert is for lunch and dinner only), and a non-alcoholic beverage, or one complete combo meal, plus one dessert (lunch and dinner), and a single serving of a soft drink.

One Snack consists of any of the following:
- Frozen ice cream novelty, ice pop, or frozen fruit bar
- Popcorn scoop (single-serving box)
- Single piece of whole fruit
- Single-serving bag of snacks
- 20-ounce bottle of soda or water
- Medium fountain soft drink
- 12-ounce coffee, tea, or hot chocolate
- Single serving of pre-packaged milk or juice

When it comes time for a meal or a snack, be sure to present your hotel room key (aka your "key to the World" card) or a MagicBand bracelet before ordering. That way your server will know to charge meals to your Disney Dining Plan. Tax is included, but gratuity is not. Please remember to tip your server!

Each time you redeem meals or snacks from the plan, your server or cashier will give you a receipt showing the remaining balance on your Dining Plan. For example, if your party of four started with 20 table-service meals and everyone in the group used one table-service meal, your receipt would indicate a balance of 16 table-service meals for the remainder of your stay.

HOT TIP

A "quick-service only" Dining Plan is a cost-efficient option. It starts at about $20 per person, per day and includes 2 quick-service meals and 1 snack a day. Everyone on the plan gets a refillable mug.

Snack credits must be redeemed at participating Walt Disney World locations. In this book, we've indicated these establishments by placing a 🐭 by each restaurant. However, as specifics may change, we recommend visiting *www.disneyworld.com* or calling 407-939-3463 for updates.

Finally, be aware that unused meals expire at midnight on your package reservation check-out date. So, on the last day of your trip, eat like there's no tomorrow! Note that table-service items are meant to be consumed on-site. In other words, please don't request a giant doggie bag.

SIGNATURE RESTAURANTS

The following "Signature" restaurants, dinner shows, and character dining experiences require guests to redeem *two credits* when using the Disney Dining Plan: Jiko—The Cooking Place, Flying Fish Cafe, California Grill, Le Cellier, Hollywood Brown Derby, Hoop-Dee-Doo Musical Revue, Mickey's Backyard Barbecue, Monsieur Paul, The Dining Room at Wolfgang Puck Cafe, Fulton's Crab House, Cítricos, Narcoossee's, The Spirit of Aloha, Artist Point, Yachtsman Steakhouse, Cinderella's Royal Table, and private dining (room service).

Magic Kingdom

A lot has changed since Walt Disney World's original theme park opened in 1971. Back then, when it came to quelling hunger pangs, it was pretty much burger or bust. Nowadays, the options are a lot more diverse—with everything from egg rolls to cinnamon rolls, smoked turkey legs to lamb stew, and clam chowder to seafood fra diavolo. Regardless of your tastes or budget, the six "lands" in the Magic Kingdom boast a bounty of palate-pleasers for the whole family.

ADVENTURELAND

🏃 Aloha Isle
`S` `$`

Switzerland meets Hawaii (hey, this *is* the Magic Kingdom) at this snack stand across from the Swiss Family Treehouse. Stop here for all things pineapple—juice, spears, floats, and the perennial favorite, the Dole Whip frozen pineapple soft-serve dessert. Also on the menu are cola and root beer floats. This spot has been around forever—they're definitely doing something right.

🏃 Sunshine Tree Terrace
`S` `$`

After you sing with the birdies in the Enchanted Tiki Room or fly on a magic carpet, you can take a break with one of the chilliest snacks in the Magic Kingdom—a refreshing Citrus Swirl (vanilla soft-serve swirled with orange slush). Ice cream floats (made with soda or coffee), espresso, and soft drinks (including soy milk) round out the menu. It's possible to get soft-serve ice cream in a cone or cup, too. A park staple, Sunshine Tree has been dishing out treats for as long as we can remember.

🏃 Tortuga Tavern
`L D S` `$-$$` 🐭

This shady stop across from Pirates of the Caribbean invites you to munch on cheesy nachos, chicken or beef burritos, and taco salads. Kids can choose cheese quesadillas. Soft drinks are also served. The venue operates seasonally, so it may not be open during your visit to the park.

FANTASYLAND

Be Our Guest Restaurant

LD $$–$$$

The atmosphere inside this colossal *Beauty and the Beast*–inspired banquet hall is impressive—it's as if Beast's Castle leaped off the screen and into Fantasyland. Lunch guests enter the Beast's parlor to place orders at touch terminals. Quick-service meals are delivered via a clever bit of technology involving an "enchanted" rose. The menu includes items such as *croque monsieur* (ham and Gruyère cheese sandwich), carved turkey on a baguette, tuna niçoise salad, grilled steak sandwich, and vegetable quiche. The portions are a bit smaller and the prices a bit steeper here than at other M.K. quick-service eateries. While many lunch guests gravitate toward the stately Ballroom, we head right for the West Wing. Just don't tell the Beast!

Dinner is a more elegant affair, with starters such as mussels Provencal, French onion soup, and *charcuterie* (cured meats). Entrées pay homage to a castle feast from the 1400s with whole roasted hen, thyme-scented pork chop, and pan-seared salmon with leek fondue and saffron potatoes. Gourmet cupcakes and mousse-filled cream puffs are finished tableside. Beer and wine are offered with the evening meal, too—a Magic Kingdom first. Reservations (for dinner) are an absolute must.

Cheshire Cafe

S $

What's appealing about this snack shack is its ability to cool you off with a lemonade, lemon slush, juice, iced coffee, and other drinks.

Cheshire Cafe serves cereal and muffins, too. On a path that borders Tomorrowland, it's easy to miss—so pay attention.

🍽️ Cinderella's Royal Table
B L D **$$$** 🐭

You don't have to be a prince or a princess to eat like one. At least, not in the Magic Kingdom. This regal establishment, tucked inside Cinderella Castle, is a high-ceilinged, majestic mead hall. It's tiny as Disney restaurants go, but there's no feeling cramped —thanks to a small number of tables and towering windows that overlook Fantasyland. It's the most upscale eatery in this kingdom, but for many, it's worth every royal penny.

Cinderella welcomes "Fairytale Dining" guests into her home for three meals a day and greets them in the lobby, while her princess friends mingle in the dining room. Breakfast favorites include lobster and crab crepes, and cream-cheese-stuffed French toast, along with traditional fare. Lunch and dinner dishes showcase seasonal ingredients, featuring savory items such as grilled lamb chops, beef tenderloin, and fish of the day. The *enormously* popular meals book up 180 days ahead. (See page 21 for details.)

Breakfast costs about $53 for adults, $34 for kids ages 3 through 9. The price includes the Princess Photo Package (see page 22). Lunch costs about $57 for adults, $35 for kids ages 3 through 9, including the Princess Photo Package. In addition to a tableside visit by Disney princesses, dinner includes an appetizer, entrée, beverage, and dessert. Dinner costs about $66 for adults, $40 for kids, and includes the photo package. Reservations are a must. Call *exactly 180 days in advance*, first thing in the morning (7 A.M.

TOUGHEST TiCKET iN TOWN

Cinderella's Royal Table character dining is—hands down—the most difficult reservation to secure at Disney World. Why? For starters, Cinderella is one popular princess. And there's the allure of dining in the castle—the most famous landmark in the world's most popular theme park. Add to that the fact that the restaurant is small (122 seats) and you end up with a supply-and-demand issue.

The good news is, thanks to a change in policy and the addition of a princess-hosted lunch, it's gotten slightly less impossible to snag a seat at Cinderella's table. Potential guests still reserve by calling 407-WDW-DINE (939-3463) 180 days ahead, but now they must pay for the meal at the same time the reservation is booked. There is no charge for infants, but they must be included in the reservation.

Expect your credit card to be charged immediately upon making the reservation. Cancellations or changes to the reservation must be made at least 24 hours ahead to receive a refund. The only one who can change or cancel a reservation is the one whose name is on the card.

Reservations cannot be transferred, and the lead name may not change.

Guests must present the credit card that was used to book the reservation, but may charge the meal to a different card or the Disney Dining Plan.

If your vacation package includes meals, you'll still have to make a reservation with a credit card. Make

Continued on page 22

Continued from page 21

sure you tell the fine folks at WDW-DINE all about your package, including the confirmation number.

Finally, a word about the (included) Photo Package: A cast member will snap a photo of your party with Cinderella inside the castle lobby. By the end of your meal, you'll receive a package including four 4-by-6-inch prints and one 6-by-8-inch print of your group, plus one 6-by-8-inch print of the castle. The Photo Package is included with the price of the meal.

Whew! That's a lot of work for one dining experience. Is it worth it? Judging by the smiles we see day in and day out, we have to say yes. Breaking bread in Cinderella's royal residence is, for many, a memory of a lifetime. (Just don't tell kids until you've secured a reservation!)

Eastern Standard Time), and keep your fingers crossed. (Guests staying at a WDW resort should read the Hot Tip on page 11.)

The Friar's Nook
LS **$**

A trip to this window, located near Storybook Treats, can yield freshly made potato chips, hot dogs, chicken nuggets, soft drinks, and snacks such as carrot cake and apple caramel dippers. Operates seasonally.

Gaston's Tavern
LDS **$** 🟡

A cozy little lodge nestled in Fantasyland's Enchanted Forest, Gaston's serves roasted pork

HOT TIP

The hours from 11 A.M. to 2 P.M., and again from about 5 P.M. to 7 P.M., are mealtime rush hours in the Magic Kingdom. Try to eat earlier or later whenever possible.

shank, hummus and chips, mixed vegetables with dip, fruit cups, sliced apples with caramel sauce, chocolate croissants, warm cinnamon rolls, and soft drinks. The specialty of this teetotaling tavern? LeFou's Brew—a not-too-sweet concoction made from frozen apple juice with a hint of toasted marshmallow and topped with all-natural passion fruit-mango foam. And, yes, Gaston really *does* use antlers in all of his decorating.

Pinocchio Village Haus
L D S $-$$ ♥

One of the better spots to target with kids in tow is Pinocchio Village Haus. It may seem small from the outside, but there are many dining rooms through that door. One room boasts picture windows that overlook the It's a Small World loading area. It's fun to watch the boats bob by as you munch on lunch. This is a good place to take kids (or picky eaters). Pinocchio offers pizza (aka flatbread), meatball subs, penne pasta, tomato basil soup, chicken nuggets, salads (Caesar and Mediterranean), fries, bread sticks, chocolate cake, cheesecake, milk shakes (chocolate or vanilla), and soft drinks. Kids' picks include mac and cheese, pasta with meatballs, and grilled cheese. This is a popular destination in a busy neighborhood—try to go a bit before or after mealtime rush hours.

🏃 Storybook Treats

S **$**

Ice cream fans will appreciate this window near the Many Adventures of Winnie the Pooh. It offers soft-serve cones and cups, hot fudge sundaes and brownie sundaes, plus milk shakes and floats.

FRONTIERLAND

🏃 The Golden Oak Outpost

L D S **$** 🐭

Located on the outskirts of Frontierland, near the Adventureland border, this little wagon can satisfy big appetites. Stop here for fried chicken breast sandwiches, chicken nuggets, fries, triple chocolate cake, carrot cake, chocolate chip cookies, soft drinks, and more. This venue operates seasonally.

🏃 Pecos Bill Cafe

L D S **$–$$** 🐭

Pecos Bill—a classic "oldie but goody"— has been feeding hungry cowpokes for more than three decades. The look has changed a bit over time, but the reliable quality of the vittles remains. Cheeseburgers, sandwiches (such as barbecue pork), chili, taco salads, chilled chicken wraps, and french fries are the staples. (If you'd rather skip the fries, ask for an à la carte version or an apple slice or corn-on-the-cob substitute.) Veggie sandwiches, steak-and-pork platters, chocolate cake, and strawberry yogurt round out the menu. Kids can choose from burgers, turkey sandwiches, or PB&J sandwiches—all with a choice of apple slices, corn-on-the-cob, or french fries.

HOT TIP

To avoid lines, make a reservation at a Magic Kingdom restaurant that takes reservations—such as Be Our Guest (dinner), Tony's Town Square, Crystal Palace, or Cinderella's Royal Table. Know that you may have to wait a few minutes once you arrive at the eatery.

What sets this spot apart from other burger establishments? Two words: fixin's bar. It's full of items with which to garnish your meal. Among them: lettuce and tomato, and freshly sautéed mushrooms and onions. Pecos Bill Cafe is one of the most popular eateries in the Magic Kingdom.

LIBERTY SQUARE

Columbia Harbour House

L D S | **$-$$** |

This lovely little spot adds some interesting (and healthy!) options to the quick-service lineup, including broccoli peppercorn salad served with chicken, grilled salmon with couscous and steamed broccoli, and the popular Lighthouse sandwich (with hummus, tomato, and broccoli slaw). You can still find fried shrimp, chicken nuggets, and clam chowder, too. For dessert there's strawberry yogurt and chocolate cake. Disney has done up this fast-food emporium with style—complete with antiques, model ships, harpoons, nautical instruments, and even lace tieback curtains. In addition to the chowder, we savor the salmon and love that Lighthouse sandwich.

HOT TIP

Is the Magic Kingdom open late today? If so, consider heading over to the Contemporary, Polynesian, Grand Floridian, or Wilderness Lodge to have an early dinner, and then return to finish the day at the Magic Kingdom. Remember to keep wearing your MagicBand bracelet if you used it for admission or keep your ticket handy for re-entry to the park. Transportation (monorail and water taxi) generally runs for one hour after the Magic Kingdom's posted closing time for the day.

Liberty Tree Tavern

L D **$$$**

Step back in time at this Early American tavern where the decor has had a tendency to outdazzle the fare. Here, the wallpaper looks as if it might have come from Colonial Williamsburg, the curtains hang from cloth loops, and the rooms are filled with mementos that might have been found in the homes of Thomas Jefferson, George Washington, and Ben Franklin. The restaurant is located across from the Hall of Presidents attraction.

The à la carte lunch menu includes salmon cakes, pot roast, turkey, salad, sandwiches, and soup. Dinner is an all-you-can-eat affair—salad, roast turkey breast, carved beef, smoked ham, mac and cheese, and more—all served family style. Dinner costs about $34 for adults, $17 for kids ages 3 through 9. Dessert is included; specialty beverages are not. Despite the tavern motif, no alcohol is served. Reservations are recommended (arrive about 20 minutes early). Disney characters do not visit here.

Sleepy Hollow

L S **$**

Often missed by guests rushing toward the
Haunted Mansion or other park hot spots, this
window has a lot to offer: waffle sandwiches
(sweet and spicy chicken or ham and Swiss),
fresh fruit, ice-cream cookie sandwiches,
cookies, funnel cakes, Mickey-shaped waffles,
and more. Also served? Coffee, hot cocoa,
and other soft drinks. Kids enjoy the Liberty
Swirl Slush (a colorful combo of strawberry
and blue raspberry slush). It's in the Hall of
Presidents neighborhood near the Liberty
Square bridge. Eat on the brick patio and get a
view of Cinderella Castle at no extra charge.

MAIN STREET, U.S.A.

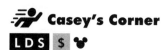

Casey's Corner

L D S **$** 🐭

Casey's is a grand slam for baseball fans—
and those who just happen to love the food
associated with America's pastime: big ol'
hot dogs and salty fries. This old-fashioned
red-and-white quick stop is on the west
side of Main Street (near the Crystal Palace
restaurant). Tables line the sidewalk, where
a ragtime pianist often tickles the ivories.
There's a back room with a table or two, plus
bleacher seating and constant screenings of
sports-themed animated shorts. The bill of
fare retains the mood—jumbo hot dogs (on
oversize multigrain rolls), corn dog nuggets,
nachos, fries, brownies, cotton candy, and soft
drinks. You gotta love a place that supplies free
cheese sauce and malt vinegar for your fries.
It's a popular spot for a late-night snack, and
a Magic Kingdom classic.

🏊 Crystal Palace
`B L D` `$$–$$$` 🐭

A landmark of sorts, this restaurant could be a Victorian garden if not for the walls and ceiling. The airy atmosphere provides a pleasant escape from the hustle and bustle of Main Street, and the all-you-can-eat buffet is a bountiful—if not terribly noteworthy—spread. Its main attraction is its character, make that *characters*: Winnie the Pooh and friends mingle with guests all day long.

Breakfast features hot and cold items, including omelets, fresh fruit, cereal, and such. The midday meal offers a salad bar, deli bar, pasta, chicken, and fish. Dinner has similar offerings: chicken, pastas, fish, carved meats, and more. Little ones love the the pint-size and kid-palate-appropriate part of the buffet.

Located toward the end of Main Street, U.S.A. (near Adventureland), the "palace" takes its architectural cues from structures that once stood in New York and London's Hyde Park, and from San Francisco's Conservatory of Flowers in Golden Gate Park. There's a Victorian-style indoor flower garden, with tables that look out on flower beds, while character topiaries greet guests at the entrance.

Cost for breakfast is about $23 for adults, $13 for children ages 3 through 9; lunch is about $25 for adults, $14 for children; dinner is about $37 for adults, $18 for children. Prices are higher during select "peak" seasons. Reservations are recommended.

🏊 Main Street Bakery
`B S` `$` 🐭

Ever popular and always crowded, this old-fashioned bakery gives off a heavenly aroma and delivers with pastries, cookies, and . . . wait for it . . . fresh-brewed Starbucks coffee. Pop in for a Frappuccino fix and the usual lineup of hot or iced coffees and teas. It's possible to get a quick breakfast and light snack items throughout the day, too.

Plaza Ice Cream Parlor

S $

This happy place for ice-cream lovers boasts the Kingdom's largest variety of hand-scooped ice cream flavors, including no-sugar-added varieties. It's great for a before-the-parade or on-the-way-out-of-the-park nosh. Little ones enjoy the Mickey Mouse kids' cone (a scoop of vanilla with chocolate ears). To keep things moving, choose flavors and desired number of scoops before jumping in line. They have sundaes and floats, too. It's busiest just before and immediately following parades and nightly fireworks presentations.

The Plaza Restaurant

LD $$ 🐭

Not to be confused with the Plaza Ice Cream Parlor, this place also boasts ice cream as the specialty of the house. Oh, wait, that *is* confusing. Here's how to differentiate: The Ice Cream Parlor is a counter-service, cones-and-cups-only establishment. The Plaza is a table-service, you-name-a-way-to-serve-ice-cream-and-they-just-might-do-it establishment. Expect sundaes, milk shakes, ice cream floats, and more. Hot and cold sandwiches (including tuna salad, fresh mozzarella, and Reubens), salads, and hamburgers are also available, as is a hearty meat loaf platter.

The charming atmosphere and the quality fare combine for a sweet dining experience. Reservations are recommended.

MAGIC KINGDOM

SPECIAL REQUESTS

Watching your salt intake? Find lactose intolerable? Most of Disney's table-service restaurants can accommodate special requirements (such as allergies to gluten or wheat, shellfish, peanuts, etc.) if requests are made at least 72 hours in advance. It's best to make your needs known when you make your advance reservations (407-WDW-DINE). Confirm your reservation and special request before arrival. Guests requiring kosher meals are encouraged to make their requests when they make their reservations. Kosher meals must be requested at least 24 hours ahead and require a credit card (the card will not be charged unless the reservation is canceled less than 24 hours prior).

Note: A 48-hour notice is needed for some table-service eateries. Kosher meals are not offered at Garden View Afternoon Tea, Teppan Edo, and Tokyo Dining.

Tony's Town Square
L D $$$ 🐭

Here it's possible to savor a fine view of Town Square while you bite into Italian specialties—pizzas, Caesar salad, sandwiches, and pasta. At dinnertime, the menu offers chicken dishes, grilled steaks, and spaghetti, along with daily specials. (If you require gluten-free pasta, just ask—Tony is happy to accommodate.) Top it off with an Italian sweet or a foamy cappuccino.

If you time it right, you can fold your napkin, pay the check, and wander onto Main Street to enjoy the fireworks from one of the best vantage points in the Magic Kingdom. Or watch *Lady and the Tramp* in the lobby. Reservations are highly recommended— especially during peak times of year.

TOMORROWLAND

Auntie Gravity's Galactic Goodies

S $

Ice cream may not seem futuristic, but chances are it'll be around at least another billion years, give or take. Located across from the Tomorrowland Speedway, Auntie G's offers up smoothies made from non-fat yogurt (strawberry-banana, orange-pineapple, and more), soft-serve ice cream, sundaes, and

TALKIN' TURKEY

Smoked turkey legs, that is. There's something barbarically compelling about gnawing on one of these popular mega-snacks. If you've had one, you know they're pretty good. Here are some things you may not know about these giant, high-calorie treats:

- Each one weighs about 1½ pounds.
- Disney guests gobble up more than 1½ million of them every year.
- The turkeys that once belonged to these legs weighed 40 to 50 pounds.
- They can be purchased at a cart in the Magic Kingdom's Frontierland and at the Lunching Pad at Rockettower Plaza in Tomorrowland.
- They cost about $9 a pop.

floats. Soft drinks are available, too. There's virtually no atmosphere in this corner of the galaxy, but we still gravitate toward the goodies.

Cosmic Ray's Starlight Cafe
L D S **$–$$** ☙

This is the largest fast-food spot in the park. Located across from Tomorrowland Speedway, it's like several quick-service counters in one. There are separate stations, with a slightly different menu offered at each.

You must wait in more than one line if you want food from different sections. Choose Bay 1 for rotisserie chicken, hot dogs, barbecue pork, or chicken sandwiches; Bay 2 for cheeseburgers, veggie burgers, and hot dogs; and Bay 3 for soup, salads, and sandwiches. Healthy sides such as green beans or cucumber salad are available. The cafe offers a kosher menu selection, too. An Audio-Animatronics (Sunny Eclipse) lounge singer performs all day.

Lunching Pad at Rockettower Plaza
S **$–$$** ☙

If it's a snack or a simple meal you're after, stop at the base of the Astro Orbiter for sweet, cream-cheese-stuffed pretzels, soda slushes, milk (regular and soy)—and specialty hot dogs (on oversize buns): Choose Philly cheesesteak, taco, or Coney Island dogs.

Tomorrowland Terrace
L D S **$–$$** ☙

Near the Plaza Restaurant, this spot serves light fare such as burgers, chicken sandwiches, and salads. Waterside tables have nice views of Cinderella Castle. Operates seasonally.

Epcot

The eclectic, international lineup of fare offered here threatens to overshadow the attractions themselves. With no fewer than 11 different countries represented in the World Showcase section of the park, Epcot provides guests with the opportunity to eat their way around the world without leaving Central Florida. Less ambitious diners will likely have their taste needs met, too—there's a bountiful food court in Epcot's Future World, as well as a smattering of simple yet satiating snack spots and quick-service locations.

FUTURE WORLD

Coral Reef (The Seas)

LD **$$$** ❤

This water-themed restaurant is all about nibbling on creatively prepared fish under the watchful eyes of their brethren. The restaurant is decorated in cool greens and blues to complement its surroundings, and every table has a panoramic view of a living coral reef; some are right up against the glass. (Don't worry: You're not actually eating Epcot residents—most of Disney's catches come fresh from fishing boats in the Atlantic each day.) Menu items run the gamut from a bounty of fresh fish and shellfish, including shrimp, mahi mahi, and salmon—prepared in a number of ways—to grilled New York strip steak and pan-seared chicken breast for those who are satisfied by simply spying on fish. And save room for the "chocolate wave" dessert. Reservations are recommended.

Electric Umbrella (Innoventions Plaza)

LDS **$-$$** ❤

This large locale is decorated in vibrant shades of blue and magenta. The restaurant is a good bet when the weather is temperate enough to allow dining at the tables on the terrace outside—or when bound for World Showcase with finicky eaters in tow. (There are lots of indoor tables, too.) Offerings include burgers, meatball subs, chicken breast pieces, tossed salads, and a vegetarian option such as Southwest black bean flatbread. Soft drinks and desserts are also available. Kids tend to enjoy the fare here.

HOLIDAY HOOPLA

During the Christmas holiday season, Epcot's World Showcase hosts a special Candlelight Processional. The show features a stirring choral concert and a reading of the Nativity Story by a celebrity narrator. The event is free (with park admission), but the general admission seating fills up as early as two hours before showtime. Rather than wait in line, we prefer to book a dining package—one that combines lunch or dinner at a World Showcase restaurant with guaranteed seating at the Processional and fireworks viewing. For information, call 407-WDW-DINE. We highly recommend this package—sure, it's a luxury, but consider it an early Christmas present for yourself!

Garden Grill (The Land)

D $$-$$$ ❤

Guests are often so distracted by the sights and the jovial hosts (Chip, Dale, and friends) that they don't realize the restaurant is actually moving. As the restaurant revolves, and it does so quite slowly, tables drift past various dioramic scenes (which are part of the attraction Living with the Land). Among the nature scenes that may be served with dinner are a thunderstorm, sandstorm, prairie, or rainforest. The scenes were designed with diners in mind and provide you with a peek into a farmhouse window that's out of viewing range of the waterborne passengers.

Chip and Dale (who may be joined by Mickey Mouse and Pluto) host the character meal here each day. The menu features turkey breast, beef tenderloin, seasonal fish, fresh vegetables (some of which are grown inside The Land pavilion), and a small selection of desserts. There is a separate kids' menu. For adults, the cost is about $35. Kids pay $17. Beverages and dessert (fresh-baked fruit crisp) are included. Meals are served family style (unlimited, communal platters for the table). Reservations are recommended. Prices may be higher during "peak" seasons.

The restaurant moves in a circle. It's imperceptible to most, but if you are highly sensitive to motion it may be best to dine in a more stationary environment.

🏃 Sunshine Seasons (The Land)
B L D S **$-$$** 🍭

It's the closest thing to a mall food court you'll find in a Walt Disney World park, but a bit more upscale. Located near the entrance to Soarin' on the pavilion's lower level, this is an ideal destination for parties who can't quite agree on any one type of fare—there's bound to be something for everyone. Tables are scattered in several areas, beneath colorful hot-air balloons. Scouting out a table can be a challenge during peak mealtimes. (There can be quite a bit of pedestrian congestion, thanks to the enormous popularity of the adjacent Soarin' attraction.)

The Sandwich Shop offers a variety of sandwiches, including a Reuben panini and an oak-grilled vegetable flatbread. **The Bakery**'s desserts include chocolate mousse cake, brownies, and ice cream bars. There is also a bountiful "grab and go" section for guests in a hurry. Among the items to choose from are sushi, hard-boiled eggs, hummus, fruit and cheese plates, salads, and snack foods.

More than 30 tons of fruits and vegetables have been grown at The Land pavilion in Epcot and served to guests dining in Walt Disney World restaurants.

EPCOT

Grill Shop offers rotisserie chicken, grilled fish, and slow-roasted pork. **The Soup & Salad Shop** serves the likes of roasted-beet and goat cheese salads and seared-tuna salad with sesame rice wine dressing. There's usually a selection of soups, too. Finally, **Wok Shop** has Mongolian beef with jasmine rice and noodle bowls (including one of the vegetarian variety).

A word of advice: It's a good idea to split up your party and stand in several lines at the same time. That'll increase your chances of actually eating together. Before you do so, select a table. That way, everyone in the party will know where to meet after they forage for their meals. It's also a nice spot to take a load off your feet while waiting for your Soarin' Fastpass window to kick in.

HOT TIP

That gift card burning a hole in your pocket? Disney Gift Cards may be redeemed at all Disney-owned-and-operated dining, shopping, and recreation locations where credit cards are accepted. If you lose track of what's left on your card, simply call the number on the back to find out.

WORLD SHOWCASE

📍🍽 Akershus Royal Banquet Hall (Norway)

B L D $$–$$$ 🐭

At Epcot's castle-like Akershus, guests are treated to authentic Norwegian cuisine. This is your chance to sample well-prepared signature dishes that rarely make their way into theme parks. Try a sampling of the Norwegian *koldtbord*, a buffet featuring smoked salmon and seafood, authentic Norwegian cheeses, and chilled salads, followed by one of the ever-changing lineups of Norwegian-inspired entrées, including seafood, beef, and poultry selections. The kids' menu offers grilled chicken, pasta and meatballs, cheese ravioli, grilled salmon, and hot dogs. Dessert is included, as are soft drinks. Don't be daunted by the strange names of some dishes; servers will explain the offerings.

Princess Storybook dining takes place here daily (breakfast, lunch, and dinner). It's an excellent alternative to Cinderella's Royal Table (which is incredibly difficult to reserve). While guests enjoy the all-you-can-eat fare, Disney princesses wander about and mingle. Belle, Jasmine, Snow White, Sleeping Beauty, and even Mulan and Ariel have made appearances. Guests get a special souvenir at meal's end—a complimentary set of photos with one of the Disney princesses. (Each set includes one 6-by-8-inch print and four 4-by-6-inch prints and is presented in a themed folder.) Note that the character appearance schedule varies. Reservations must be made with a credit card. Changes and cancellations must be made at least 48 hours ahead to avoid a $10 per person charge.

🍴 Biergarten (Germany)
L **D** | **$$–$$$** | 🐭

EPCOT

Year in and year out, this place makes us happy. It's a reasonably priced, all-you-can-eat buffet of traditional German cuisine set in a charming courtyard. Adding to the fun are communal tables and live entertainment (at lunch and dinner). It's pretty much Oktoberfest year-round.

The hearty, varied buffet features a selection of sausages, rotisserie chicken, spaetzle, chicken schnitzel, potato salad, cucumber salad, and many other German specialties. Wash it all down with soft drinks, German wine, or a stein of beer (suds purists may grouse at the limited selection of beer). Among the dessert options is apple strudel with vanilla sauce.

The entertainment consists of occasional appearances by traditional Bavarian musicians—each clad in lederhosen or dirndl—who play accordions, cowbells, a musical saw, and a harp-like stringed instrument known as the "wooden laughter." Performances take place at scheduled times in the dining room. Diners are usually invited to join the fun on the dance floor. Because entertainment is intermittent, there's plenty of time to enjoy the pleasant setting. Reservations are recommended, particularly during peak times of year (summer and school holidays).

🥐 Les Halles Boulangerie Patisserie (France)
L **D** **S** | **$–$$** | 🐭

For some guests, a visit to Epcot is incomplete without stopping by this ever-popular pastry shop (which recently moved and expanded in size), tucked toward the back of the France pavilion. Crowds are forever lining up to consume the flaky croissants, éclairs, fruit tarts, and chocolate mousse. It's also possible to indulge in a cheese plate, quiche, or a ham and cheese croissant. The baguettes are *magnifique*. Wash it all down with cappuccino, hot chocolate, or a glass of champagne.

The treats were selected under the management of the chefs who were the culinary brains behind the Chefs de France restaurant not far away. This has become a favorite snacking stop among Epcot veterans. Your best bet is to stop here as soon as World Showcase opens or during IllumiNations, the nightly fireworks show (but you can't see the show from here). Note that the space formerly occupied by this shop has morphed into an ice cream and sorbet shop.

Chefs de France (France)

L D $$$–$$$$

"Bright lights, big dining room" describes this airy Parisian brasserie. With some of France's best chefs responsible for this nouvelle French kitchen, the results are rewarding. The menu features fresh ingredients readily available from Florida purveyors, though the restaurant

ONE-STOP SWEET SHOP

A delectable addition to the World Showcase landscape, the Germany pavilion's Karamell Küche is sure to satisfy your sweet tooth–provided that you're a fan of fresh, gooey caramel draped or drizzled over chocolate, cookies, crunchy apples, and much, much more.

imports as many key ingredients from France as possible.

The offerings are French, but the foundation of the menu is nouvelle cuisine, which involves lighter sauces using less cream and butter than in classic French cooking. Menu items include broiled salmon, beef short ribs, and all-natural roasted chicken. Soups and appetizers such as onion soup, lobster bisque, and escargot are all-day staples. Crème brûlée and chocolate profiteroles (cream puffs) are dessert favorites. Wine pairings are recommended from a well-rounded list.

Chefs de France is one of the most expensive World Showcase eateries. Still, given its perennial popularity, many guests agree it's worth the splurge. Reservations are a must.

🏃 Cool Post (between Germany and China)
S $

As its name suggests, this place specializes in all things cool: soft-serve ice cream, beer, and soft drinks—plus hot dogs.

🏃 Fife & Drum Tavern (American Adventure)
L D S $-$$ 🐭

Hear ye, hear ye! Head to this snack stand on World Showcase Promenade (across from the America Gardens Theater) for jumbo turkey legs, popcorn, hot pretzels, frozen slushes, root beer floats, soft drinks, and American beer.

🏃 Katsura Grill (Japan)
L D S $ 🐭

Easy to miss, what with its out-of-the-way location, Katsura is a nice spot to go to escape the masses and savor a simple meal. The eatery sits beside a small garden. The fare includes Asian favorites ranging from sushi to Japanese beef curry, teriyaki and udon noodles, *edamame*, curry rice, and miso soup. Drinks include green tea, Kirin beer, and sake. For dessert, choose a cookie, ice cream (green tea or strawberry), or a fluffy piece of matcha roll cake (also made with green tea).

✈ Kringla Bakeri og Kafe (Norway)

L D S $-$$ ❦

This bake shop serves *kringles*, sweet pretzels reserved for special occasions in Norway; cloudberry horns, flaky pastries filled with cream and cloudberries; *lefse* (potato bread with cinnamon sugar); and sandwiches such as open-faced smoked salmon on multigrain toast, plus roast beef, or ham and apple. It's possible to get a small salad or fruit cup, too. Our favorite menu item? The vegetable tart. Yum! There are no seats in the bakery, but guests may eat in a shaded outdoor area.

✈ La Cantina de San Angel (Mexico)

L D S $-$$ ❦

Located directly across from Mexico's pyramid, this lagoonside eatery serves traditional Mexican fare. Expect selections such as cheese empanadas, fresh guacamole and tortilla chips, nachos heaped with toppings, and beef or chicken tacos, plus caramel churros and frozen fruit pops. This is a prime spot from which to view the evening's presentation of IllumiNations (it gets mighty crowded just before showtime). Beer and margaritas are available, as are soft drinks.

🍽 La Hacienda de San Angel (Mexico)

LD **$$–$$$** ❤

The Mexico pavilion's newest eatery, La Hacienda has a striking exterior that was designed to look like a south-of-the-border home. The attention to detail continues inside, with original artwork and lighting fixtures, and chairs and tables that were crafted in Mexico.

Most tables have a view of the lagoon, but seats near the windows double as front row seats for the evening's presentation of IllumiNations—Reflections of Earth. The dining room is a hot ticket for the nightly

FOOD AND WINE FESTIVAL

Once a year, Epcot's hopping dining scene expands exponentially in what's known as the International Food and Wine Festival. The event, which usually runs from late September through early November, is a celebration of the flavors of dozens of nations. Those countries without permanent stations at World Showcase set up temporary displays from which authentic samples of food and wine are sold. The samples range in price from about $3 to $8. It's possible to eat and drink your way around the world for about the same price as some table-service restaurants.

The festival also features demonstrations from top chefs, as well as wine and cooking seminars. For specifics, visit *www.disneyworld.com* or call 407-824-4321. Make reservations as early as you can—this is one popular festival.

show, with music pumped inside. (If your table isn't ideally situated, there's usually standing room with a good view of IllumiNations.)

Appetizers include warm chips and two salsas (one mild, one with zing), mini-tacos, black bean soup, and roasted sweet peppers with lime and sea salt, served with chorizo sausage. There are two entrées—one beef, one seafood—that are meant for sharing (though you may not want to). Flank steak or shrimp tacos, pork, chicken, and grilled tilapia dishes round out the menu. Reservations are recommended.

Le Cellier Steakhouse (Canada)

L D **$$–$$$**

We love retreating to this peaceful wine-cellar-like spot, a favorite place for a hearty meal. The restaurant has low ceilings, lantern light, and stone walls, all of which contribute to the atmosphere.

There's a full menu of tempting items, starting with a bread basket that includes a pretzel, plus sourdough, and whole-grain creations. Considered a "signature" restaurant for both lunch and dinner, the steakhouse specializes in high-quality beef, from grilled Wagyu short rib to a New York strip and grilled bone-in ribeye. The filet mignon with white truffle-butter sauce is a real crowd-pleaser. Many choose to start with longtime favorite cheddar cheese soup made with Moosehead beer, but the classic poutine fries (fries with cheddar, truffle salt, and red wine reduction) is a popular starter, too. Canadian beers and wines make for memorable pairings. Reservations are a must—this is an extremely popular and relatively tiny restaurant. Disney Dining Plan participants must cash in two table-service meals per person to dine here. (We think it's worth it.)

Liberty Inn (The American Adventure)

L D S $-$$ 🐭

While it may seem like the flavors of the United States get short shrift when it comes to representation at Epcot, that's not the case here. True, there's no America-oriented table-service restaurant at World Showcase, though the Garden Grill over in Future World proudly serves up platters of Americana. On the international side of the park, Liberty Inn dishes out what many think of as American food: burgers, chili cheese dogs, and fries. Also on the menu are (yummy) black bean vegetable burgers, grilled chicken flatbreads, chicken nuggets, salads, sandwiches, and desserts (think baked apple pie or a brownie). This is a good choice for kids and picky eaters.

Lotus Blossom Cafe (China)

L D S $-$$ 🐭

The fare may not live up to the splendor of the pavilion, but if you crave a quick Chinese food fix, this place, adjacent to the shopping gallery in the China pavilion, offers orange chicken, beef noodle soup bowl, salad, egg rolls, pot stickers, shrimp fried rice, and more. There is a covered outdoor seating area.

Marrakesh (Morocco)

L D S $$-$$$ 🐭

It's not every day that you can slip into an exquisitely tiled Moroccan palace and be entertained by belly dancers and musicians as you polish off a plate of Moroccan cuisine. Want to know how authentic this place is? The king of Morocco sent craftspeople to Epcot to make sure they were creating a real Moroccan atmosphere. (Unfortunately, the cuisine plays second fiddle to the surroundings.) The menu includes roast lamb, chicken brochette, beef shish kebab, and couscous. Sampler platters are available. Reservations are recommended, but it's usually possible to get in without much of a wait.

📯 Mitsukoshi (Japan)

LD $$$ 🂠

Within the sprawling Mitsukoshi complex (which is run by the Japanese company of the same name), there are two options:

Tokyo Dining fills a chic, colorful space in the Mitsukoshi building. If you're in the mood for sushi, sashimi, tempura, grilled chicken, salmon, or filet mignon, head here. For something unusual, try the grilled freshwater eel or braised pork belly slowly cooked in sake. It's possible to munch on *edamame* and indulge in sake and Japanese beer, among other drinks. (We wish they had low-sodium soy sauce, but we did get extra wasabi when we requested it.) A few window-side tables allow a view of the nightly presentation of IllumiNations. Reservations are recommended.

Teppan Edo, Tokyo Dining's lively neighbor, fills the space formerly occupied by Teppanyaki Dining Room. As with its predecessor, guests here sit around a large *teppan* grill and watch as a nimble chef demonstrates just how quickly enough chicken, beef, seafood, and vegetables to feed eight people can be chopped, seasoned, and stir-fried. Teppan Edo entrées are sizzling and satisfying. Soups, salads, sushi, desserts, and cocktails (including beer and sake) are also on the menu. Don't wear your finest attire: There's always the potential for a little splattering here and there. Reservations are recommended.

🍽️ Monsieur Paul (France)

D **$$$$** 🐭

This elegant bistro—upscale but less formal than its predecessor, Bistro de Paris—is decorated with mementos of Chef Paul Bocuse's extra-ordinary culinary honors. Located one flight above Chefs de France, Monsieur Paul captures classic French architecture with bright colors and a touch of modernism.

The menu (crafted by Chef Francesco Santin, who worked with Chef Bocuse in his restaurant in Lyon, France, for 15 years) features dishes such as *soup aux truffles* (black winter truffle and beef broth soup); Maine lobster with diced vegetables, bisque, and rice pilaf; herb-crusted rack of lamb niçoise-style tart, and seared scallops with black truffle spaghettini. You might want to stroll around the World Showcase promenade to walk off your meal—and your warm Grand Marnier dessert soufflé. The wine list is *très* French. Reservations are recommended.

🍽️ Nine Dragons (China)

LD **$$$** 🐭

This stop on Epcot's varied international restaurant tour offers family-style meals prepared in provincial Chinese cooking styles. On the appetizer menu, expect enticing items such as lightly spiced napa salad, spring rolls, pot stickers, and dumplings. Entrées include sweet-and-sour pork, spicy kung pao chicken, vegetable stir-fry, peppery shrimp, five-spiced fish, and Chinese barbecue.

A nice variety of imported teas, beers, and wines is available. Dessert selections include red-bean ice cream, caramel-ginger ice cream, banana cheesecake egg roll, and ginger cake. Reservations are recommended.

Refreshment Port (Canada)

S **$**

Located near Canada, this stand offers smoothies, chicken sandwiches, fried shrimp, fries, soft drinks, and soft-serve ice cream. It's a good spot for a quick snack.

Rose & Crown Pub & Dining Room (United Kingdom)

L D S **$$–$$$** 🐭

Don't let the word "pub" throw you. While this place serves up some of the best brews on Disney property, its dining area is also known for such crowd-pleasing dishes as crispy fish and chips and bangers and mash (sausages with mashed potatoes), with a side of mushy peas.

Dessert options include sticky toffee pudding and cake. Bass ale from England and Harp lager and Guinness stout, both from Ireland, are on tap.

The pub section of the Rose & Crown serves such snacks as a U.K. cheese plate and fish and chips—along with all the brews noted above and traditional British mixed drinks. A piano player is sometimes on hand to entertain revelers. The pub section also spills out onto the promenade—where the first-come, first-snagged waterside tables make for a nice spot

HOT TIP

La Cava de Tequila, inside Mexico's pyramid, is a cozy lounge featuring 95 varieties of tequila and a few mouth-watering appetizers. It's a great spot for a light meal. There are a few tables, but the bar is standing room only. Reservations are not accepted here. Weekends are busiest.

to sip a drink and/or enjoy a snack from a nearby stand. Reservations are not available in the pub, but are recommended for the restaurant.

🍽 San Angel Inn (Mexico)
LD $$$ 🔸

The lights are low, the mood is romantic, and there is a smoking volcano tableside. If that's not enchantment enough, there's also a moonlit river. It all takes place inside the pyramid that serves as the Mexico pavilion.

Here you'll find traditional Mexican fare from margaritas to tacos and enchiladas. The eatery also offers fresh fish, poultry, and meat dishes. To start, there's *tlacoyos de chilorio* (corn cakes topped with refried beans, pork, cheese, sour cream, and green tomatillo sauce) and *tacos de filete* (grilled beef tenderloin served on a soft flour tortilla with chipotle pepper sauce, scallions, and avocados). Entrées include pan-seared tilapia; *carne asada a la Tampiqueña* (grilled tenderloin with cheese enchilada, black refried beans, red bell pepper, onion, rice, and guacamole); and pork tenderloin with a sauce of pumpkin, chiles, and almonds; plus soup and salads.

The desserts may be unfamiliar to diners, but are worth trying. The *crepas de cajeta* (warm crepes with caramel sauce and toasted almonds) are among the more popular treats. Beer and margaritas make good accompaniments. Reservations are recommended.

🏃 Sommerfest (Germany)
LDS $-$$ 🔸

Here, speedy sustenance takes such classic forms as bratwurst, frankfurters, and soft pretzels (if they're dry, we send 'em back). For dessert, there's Black Forest cake and apple strudel. The shaded outdoor seating area sports a festive mural. German wine and beer are offered, too.

🛫 Tangierine Cafe (Morocco)
L D S $-$$ 🐭

Named for the Moroccan city of Tangier, this casual spot serves (unremarkable) Mediterranean specialties—lentil salad, hummus, and tabbouleh, as well as rotisserie chicken and lamb presented as sandwiches (served on Moroccan bread) and combo platters (including a vegetarian option). Specialty coffees and pastries are available.

HOT TIP

The newest addition to the Italy pavilion is Gusto, a wine bar that transports guests to an ancient Italian wine cellar. Tutto Italia's next-door neighbor offers more than 200 wines, including grappa; Italian beers and specialty drinks; coffee concoctions; and a small-plate menu. Reservations are not accepted—come in the afternoon for the smallest crowds. Salute!

🍽 Tutto Italia (Italy)
L D S $$-$$$ 🐭

The menu has made Tutto Italia one of the most popular World Showcase restaurants, and the outdoor tables make it one of the more pleasant spots for dining at Epcot (when the weather cooperates, that is). Traditional starters such as fried calamari, fresh mozzarella with tomatoes and basil, and Caesar salad can make a meal in and of themselves. However, we recommend sampling the fresh pastas, made here daily: spaghetti, tagliatelle, lasagna, and more. Fish, pork, and chicken entrées round out the menu. At lunchtime, paninis are also an option—as is a selection of desserts.

Via Napoli (Italy)

L D S **$$**

Finally! A place to get pizza at Epcot's Italy. Located toward the back of the pavilion, this 300-seat spot serves Neapolitan-style pizza, pastas, salads, sandwiches, soft drinks (including a mix of grape and orange juices and a bit of fizzy water called Graspia), and a selection of wines. How serious are they about pizza? They import the flour from Italy and select water so the crust tastes as authentically Neapolitan as possible. Reservations are recommended.

Yorkshire County Fish Shop (United Kingdom)

L D S **$**

A perfect choice for a snack or a light lunch, this stand offers scrumptious fish and chips. (Don't forget the malt vinegar.) Soda, iced tea, light lemonade, Bass ale and Harp lager are also available. For a snack, there's English sugar cookies and bags of potato chips.

HOT TIP

If you plan to see IllumiNations, know that the show takes place nightly at 9 P.M. Try to time it so your evening meal winds up no later than 8:45 P.M.—and tell your server when you arrive.

HOT TIP

For a sweet treat, visit the new L'Artisan des Glaces, Artisan Ice Cream & Sorbet, in Epcot's France pavilion. It offers 16 flavors of ice cream and sorbet—all made with simple, fresh ingredients: milk, sugar, cream, eggs, and fruit. How cool is that?!

CHECK, PLEASE!

Paying for a meal at Disney World is a piece of cake—especially if you have a Disney resort ID or MagicBand bracelet (and back it up with a major credit card upon check-in). Both are accepted by most restaurants on WDW property. Notable exceptions: eateries at the Swan and Dolphin resorts, some Downtown Disney spots, the resorts on Hotel Plaza Boulevard, and some snack carts. Simply scan your bracelet or hand your resort ID to the waiter or cashier, sign the bill (don't forget to add a tip where appropriate), and the charge will appear on your hotel statement when you check out.

Of course, there are many alternative ways to pay the piper. In addition to United States currency, traveler's checks and major credit cards are accepted in most non-snack-cart locations. Foreign currency is always a no-no. Disney currency (aka Disney Dollars) works like cash in all Disney-owned-and-operated venues. Disney Gift Cards are accepted at most WDW-owned-and-operated establishments. (If you plan to pay with a gift card, tell your server when you place your order.)

Disney's Hollywood Studios

Lights, camera, lunch! This theme park, designed to resemble a working Hollywood backlot circa the 1940s, tackles the role of feeding guests with style and whimsy. Here you can sit in a classic car and enjoy a meal at a drive-in, rub elbows with the beautiful people at a reproduction of the Hollywood Brown Derby, and play the part of sitcom kid as you're served by "Mom" or "Dad" at the 50's Prime Time Cafe (no elbows on the table, please!). While the attention to theming is obvious, it doesn't upstage the fare. So grab a napkin, and get ready for your close-up.

ABC Commissary

L D S | **$–$$** ♥

Located near the Chinese Theatre, this spot has shaken up the menu a few times of late. Most recently, it featured fish and chips, fried shrimp, cheeseburgers, couscous, quinoa and arugula salad with chicken or salmon, and an Asian-style salad. Dessert items include strawberry parfait and chocolate mousse. Soft drinks, beer, and wine are served. Note that breakfast is no longer offered here. The restaurant is huge and does indeed resemble an actual studio commissary. We could do without the ads for ABC shows, which play on a continuous loop from TVs scattered throughout the dining area. Enough already!

Backlot Express

L D S | **$–$$** ♥

Designed to look like a crafts shop on an old studio backlot, this eatery is near the Star Tours attraction. The indoor seating areas carry out the prop-shop theme, with paint-speckled floors, car engines, and various other spare prop parts. Outdoor tables are situated amid plants and trees. Menu offerings include burgers, chicken nuggets, hot dogs, grilled turkey and cheese sandwiches, grilled veggie sandwiches (our favorite), and salads. For dessert, there's no-sugar-added strawberry parfait. Soft drinks and beer are available.

50's Prime Time Cafe

L D | **$$–$$$** ♥

This retreat to the era of *I Love Lucy* is an amusing amalgam of comfort food, kitschy 1950s-style kitchen nooks, and attentive servers of the "No talking with your mouth full"

FANTASMIC! DINNER PACKAGE

Guests who make dining arrangements at their Disney resort or at any of the parks can take advantage of the Fantasmic! Dining Opportunity Special. Reserved seating for the evening's performance of Fantasmic! comes with the meal at no extra cost.

Why book the package? Besides guaranteeing a seat for dinner (lunch is offered seasonally), it ensures that you will get seating for Fantasmic! without having to wait in line. This is critical—since guests start lining up for the show as much as two hours ahead. With the package, you can have a relaxing dinner and head over to the show shortly before it starts.

Call 407-939-3463 for info or to book a "dinner and a show" package. At press time, the Hollywood Brown Derby, Hollywood & Vine, and Mama Melrose's Ristorante Italiano were participating in the program. (The Fantasmic! Dining Opportunity may be available for walk-ins, but we highly recommend booking it in advance—you've got nothin' to lose!)

ilk. Nostalgia abounds, with more cookie jars than you could shake an Oreo at, all meant to bring you back to childhood of yesteryear; even the dessert menu is read on a View-Master, and TVs broadcast black-and-white clips from favorite fifties comedies (all related to food). Guests are waited on by "Mom" (and other family members) with considerable enthusiasm: They encourage everyone to keep their elbows off the table, eat their vegetables, and clean their plates (or no dessert!). Misbehave and you may have to stand in the corner (the 1950s "time out").

Adding to the appeal is the menu, which is packed with comfort foods. For openers, there's a choice of homemade chicken noodle soup or onion rings. Specialties of the house include magnificent meat loaf, served with mashed potatoes and vegetables; fried chicken; and old-fashioned pot roast. There are Caesar salads and chicken pot pie, too. Milk shakes, ice-cream sodas, and root beer floats are filling accompaniments. And when you've finished everything on your plate, you may order dessert. Standouts include s'mores—graham crackers topped with chocolate and toasted marshmallows—sundaes, apple crisp, and no-sugar-added cheesecake topped with whipped cream and strawberry sauce. A full bar is available. Guests of all ages love this place. Reservations are recommended.

Hollywood & Vine
B L D **$$$**

The exterior is Art Deco, and the interior conjures up memories of a 1950s American diner—forged out of stainless steel with pink accents. It's next door to the 50's Prime Time Cafe, just off Hollywood Boulevard.

The buffet breakfast and lunch, known

BABY NEEDS

Babies. They're a needy lot. Fortunately, most of the requisite supplies can be found somewhere at Disney World—if you know where to look. Formula and jarred food can be purchased at the Baby Care Center in each of the theme parks and at every WDW resort. Most restaurants have kids' menus with toddler-friendly food (mac and cheese, chicken nuggets, and the like).

If your baby is partial to a specific formula or brand of food, consider shipping a box of it to your hotel before you leave home. Keep in mind that there are several grocery stores near Disney World. If you'll have a car, it is worth the trip (a guest relations clerk can offer directions). The selections are more varied, as are the prices. Stash perishables in an in-room refrigerator—they are standard in all Disney-owned-and-operated resorts. It's best to request one when you make your reservation. Some other points of interest regarding baby diners at WDW:

- Most eateries have high chairs and booster seats. Request one when you make your restaurant reservation.
- Stroller use inside restaurants is discouraged. Park it outside.
- WDW restaurants are often chilly. Be sure to pack a sweater or blanket.
- Be it a fast-food or table-service restaurant, bring toys to keep the little one(s) busy.
- The following resorts have 24-hour snack bars: Grand Floridian, Dolphin, Polynesian, Wyndham, and Buena Vista

Continued on page 58

> **Continued from page 57**
>
> Palace (on Hotel Plaza Boulevard). The middle-of-the-night pickings may be slim, but milk and cereal are served 'round the clock.
>
> - If you'd like a quiet spot to nurse an infant, head to a Baby Care Center in any of the theme parks. They all have rooms with rocking chairs.
> - If you're headed for a long day in a theme park, pack simple, healthy snacks for toddlers.
> - To make your dining experience less harried, consider feeding your baby before you get to the restaurant.

as Disney Junior Play 'n Dine, are character affairs featuring June from *Little Einsteins*, Special Agent Oso, Jake the Never Land pirate, and Handy Manny. The morning meal includes an omelet station, Mickey waffles, frittatas, fruit, and pastries. Lunch offers a pasta station, plus items such as salmon with maple mustard glaze, grilled polenta with sun-dried tomatoes, and salads. Dinner, which is character-free, also features carved meats, peel-and-eat shrimp, and mussels. Some soft drinks are included, as is a dessert buffet which includes a chocolate fountain. Reservations are recommended.

Hollywood Brown Derby
LD **$$–$$$**

The Studios' most gracious dining is found at this faithful revival of the original *cause célèbre*, which opened on Hollywood and Vine in 1926. Dressed to the nines in chandeliers and celebrity caricatures, the restaurant stokes the appetite with its ever-so-finely chopped signature Cobb salad (invented by Brown Derby owner Bob Cobb) and grapefruit cake —a Brown Derby institution. Some of the fare is a bit highbrow (and high-priced) for the theme park crowd, but if you're up for a splurge, this spot is sure to rise to the occasion. We recommend the seafood cioppino; the filet mignon gets good marks, too.

The slightly formal atmosphere is not likely to enchant most kids, but youngster-friendly fare is available. The New World wine list is excellent. Reservations are recommended.

🍽 Mama Melrose's Ristorante Italiano

L D **$$–$$$** 🐭

This pleasant Italian restaurant (with a California twist) is located in a large warehouse that has been converted into a dining room. Flatbreads are prepared in a wood-burning oven. The menu also features grilled fish, house-made pasta, and vegetarian options. Dishes include seafood arrabbiata, charred strip steak, wild mushroom and arugula flatbread, and oven-baked chicken parmigiana, plus soups and salads. The wine list includes selections from California and Italy. Reservations are recommended.

HOT TIP

If you can stand to miss the evening's performance of Fantasmic! (Disney's Hollywood Studios nighttime spectacular), consider dining in one of the park's popular eateries during the show.

Min and Bill's Dockside Diner

S $

Mmm . . . milk shakes. 'Nuf said. In addition to some of the greatest, thickest chocolate and vanilla shakes in the World, Min and Bill's waterside snack spot also serves Italian sausage sandwiches with pepper and onions, hot dogs in pretzel rolls, chicken Caesar sandwiches, cookies, soft drinks, frozen lemonade, and domestic beer. To find it, look for the boat with the line to board, er, buy.

FYI: *Min and Bill* was a 1930s feature film (one of the first talkies) that took place on a waterfront. Hence, the lakefront locale.

Oasis Canteen

S $

A tiny tin shack that sits beside the Indiana Jones Epic Stunt Spectacular, the Oasis Canteen dispenses funnel cakes topped with strawberries, vanilla ice cream, powdered sugar, or cinnamon; soft-serve ice cream in waffle cones or cups (chocolate, vanilla, or swirl); bottled water; and domestic draft beer.

Pizza Planet

L D S $-$$ 🐭

Located inside a kid-magnet arcade, this is a counter-service spot with a limited but youngster-friendly menu. Select from simple individual pizzas (vegetarian, cheese, or pepperoni), meatball subs, salads (chicken and garden), fresh-baked chocolate chip cookies, apple slices, Mickey's crispy treats, cappuccino, and soft drinks (including chocolate milk and apple juice). There is seating just outside the door.

While the Sci-Fi Dine-In Theater has tables that can accommodate guests who use wheelchairs, there aren't many. Be sure to request such a table when you make your reservations—and confirm it before you go; 407-WDW-DINE (939-3463).

  Sci-Fi Dine-In Theater

L D $$–$$$ ❤

A convincing re-creation of a drive-in theater, the atmosphere here is completely absorbing. The tables are actually flashy, 1950s-era cars, complete with fins and whitewalls. Stars twinkle overhead in the "night sky," and drive-in theater speakers are mounted beside each car. Most seats are within cars, with most featuring front- and backseat counters facing front. Not terribly conducive to meaningful table talk, but ideal for viewing the large movie screen, where a 45-minute compilation of the best (and worst) of science-fiction trailers and cartoons plays in a continuous loop. There are a couple of traditional tables within oversize cars—if this is your preference, make that known when you book the table and expect to wait a bit when you arrive.

Selections include Reuben sandwiches, chicken sandwiches, burgers, and shrimp pasta. Kids enjoy the macaroni and cheese. Desserts include cheesecake, milk shakes, and ice cream sundaes. It's popular with all ages, but some kids get spooked by the monsters in the movie clips. There are a few tables that accommodate guests using wheelchairs. Reservations are recommended.

Starring Rolls Cafe
B L S **$–$$** 🍴

In a hurry? Head here to get the day off to a quick start, or take a nice coffee break. Pastries, muffins, croissants, and whole fruits are sold at this sweet-smelling shop. Coffee (beans are ground on-site), tea, and soft drinks are also served. For lunch, sandwiches, sushi, and wine are available. (Get there early if you really want sushi—they're always sold out by the time we arrive.) This spot closes at 4 P.M.

Studio Catering Co.
L D S **$–$$** 🍴

Next to the Honey, I Shrunk the Kids Movie Set Adventure, this spot offers sandwiches (vegetarian, buffalo chicken, turkey club, and more) and Greek salads. There is a full bar serving specialty libations, too.

Sunset Ranch Market
B L D S **$–$$** 🍴

A celebration of California's outdoor lifestyle, this open-air cluster of snack stands has something for everyone. **Rosie's All-American Cafe** sells cheeseburgers, veggie burgers, chicken breast nuggets, salads, and soups. **Catalina Eddie's** offers pizzas, hot Italian deli-style sandwiches, salads, chocolate-fudge cake, and carrot cake. Fruit, carrots, pretzels, granola bars, pickles, soft drinks, and frozen margaritas are available at **Anaheim Produce**. **Toluca Legs Turkey Co.** serves turkey legs. **Hollywood Scoops Ice Cream** offers creamy treats (including one sugar-free flavor). **Fairfax Fare** features smoked specialties, including ribs and chicken, hot dogs, and breakfast selections (pastries and sandwiches).

Disney's Animal Kingdom

Walt Disney World's nature-oriented theme park is ideal for grazers: with more than a dozen spots to nosh, it may not be strong on table service (there are three such eateries), but it takes "quick service" quite seriously. When your stomach starts growling like the beasts at the Kilimanjaro Safaris attraction, consider the top-notch Tusker House and Flame Tree Barbecue. Not only do they offer mouth-watering meals, but they serve them in some of the fanciest theme park dining environments around.

Anandapur Ice Cream Truck

`S` `$`

This ice-cream truck doesn't actually move, but the Asia-based vehicle does deliver chilly treats. Ice cream is available by the cone or in a soda float.

Dino-Bite Ice Cream & Treats

`S` `$` 🐭

In DinoLand U.S.A., next door to Restaurant-osaurus, is a small stand that offers ice cream (hand-dipped scoops, sundaes, floats, etc.), chocolate chip cookies, chips, churros, and other snacks throughout the day.

Flame Tree Barbecue

`L` `D` `S` `$-$$` 🐭

If you can't find this eatery, just follow your nose. Because when the kitchen is cooking, the scent is compelling. It serves up a selection of barbecued sandwiches and platters, all wood roasted. Sample the mild, tomato-based barbecue sauce or the spicy, mustard-based Carolina-style sauce with your chicken, pulled pork, or hickory-smoked St. Louis ribs. Disney's ovens produce 1,200 pounds at a time. Smoked turkey breast sandwiches, BBQ chicken salads, fruit plates (served with honey yogurt), fries, onion rings, and chocolate or Key lime mousse round out the options. Platters are served with baked beans and/or corn-on-the-cob. French fries and onion rings are also offered. Beer, wine, and soft drinks are served. There's outdoor seating along the river (which is quite lovely when it's not 98 degrees). If Flame Tree isn't serving, the tables are still open for use. It's located on Discovery Island, near DinoLand.

🏃 Harambe Fruit Market

`S` `$`

Sometimes, a crunchy apple is just what the doctor—or the hungry theme park guest—ordered. Apples, among other healthy snacks, are available at this fruit stand near the entrance to Kilimanjaro Safaris. Water and sports drinks are sold here, too.

🏃 Kusafiri Coffee Shop & Bakery

`B S` `$`

The bakery next to Tusker House provides a steady stream of fresh-from-the-oven treats such as croissants, muffins, and other snacks, plus cappuccino and espresso.

🏃 Pizzafari

`L D S` `$–$$` 🐭

This big, colorful dining area has no-nonsense fare that tends to please young palates. Plain, pepperoni, and veggie pizzas; chicken and vegetable pasta salad; and hot Italian-style sandwiches are all on the menu. Animal murals decorate the walls of this restaurant, located on Discovery Island.

🍽 Rainforest Cafe

`B L D S` `$$–$$$`

Animal Kingdom's original table-service restaurant is located at its front entrance. The atmosphere blends well with the theme park it borders. Environmentally conscious cuisine includes items like Planet Earth Pasta and the Plant Sandwich. (The Big Blue Crab Delight—creamy dip loaded with crabmeat and served with tortilla chips—is consistently enjoyable.) There's no net-caught fish on the menu, nor beef from countries that destroy rainforest land to raise cattle. Fish tanks, tropical decor, and the occasional thunderstorm add to the ambience (and noise level). Kids thrive here.

The restaurant and bar are accessible from inside and outside Animal Kingdom, so admission to the park isn't necessary to enter, though there is a charge for parking. Reservations are recommended for all meals.

WATER PARK DINING

Disney's duo of water parks, Typhoon Lagoon and Blizzard Beach, provides plenty of opportunities to defy Mom's plea to wait an hour to splash after you nosh. The fare is limited to the quick-service kind (who wants a sit-down meal in a soggy swimsuit?), and the quality of the offerings has been stepped up a bit of late. Typhoon Lagoon offers hot Italian sandwiches, fresh fruit bowls, meatball subs, and more.

At Blizzard Beach, we're partial to the tomato-mozzarella sandwich and hot dogs wrapped in a soft pretzel. Snacks are sold at spots with names like Typhoon Tilly's (♥), Leaning Palms (♥), and Avalunch (♥). Frozen drink specialties flow at Let's Go Slurpin' (Typhoon Lagoon) and at Blizzard Beach's Polar Bear Pool Bar.

Some folks prefer to pack a picnic lunch. Coolers may be brought into both parks, but alcoholic beverages and glass containers may not.

🏃 Restaurantosaurus

`L D S` `$-$$` 🐭

Hang a right once you enter DinoLand U.S.A. and you'll discover this spot. A fishing lodge turned commissary for student paleontologists, it offers fast food at lunch and dinner: burgers, chicken nuggets, veggie subs, chicken BLT salad, and hot dogs—plus fries, apple slices, chocolate mousse, and cheesecake in a glass.

🏃 Royal Anandapur Tea Co.

`S` `$`

After hiking through Africa to get to Asia, guests can build up quite a thirst. That's where this exotic tea stand comes in handy. Located near the Yak & Yeti, this spot has a variety of iced and hot teas, fruit smoothies, specialty coffees, and sweet treats.

🏃 Tamu Tamu Refreshments

`S` `$` 🐭

This window dispenses cheeseburgers, roast beef sandwiches, quinoa salad, and shakes. There's a seating nook next door. It's in Harambe, across from Tusker House.

🏃 Trilo-Bites

`S` `$`

This little cabin, located just inside the entrance to DinoLand, sells smoked turkey legs, frozen lemonade, and soft drinks.

🍽 Tusker House

`B L D S` `$-$$` 🐭

The Tusker House fare—which is offered buffet style—is head, shoulders, and antlers above the rest. It's on the left side of Harambe, just over the bridge from Discovery Island. Donald Duck fans are especially pleased with the addition of Donald's Safari Breakfast and Dinner buffets. It's offered daily and includes visits from the aforementioned fowl, plus Mickey, Daisy, and Goofy. Breakfast runs from 8 A.M. until 10:30 A.M., while lunch and dinner are offered from 11:15 A.M. till the park's posted closing time. Reservations are recommended. The Kusafiri Coffee Shop & Bakery operates from a window outside.

Yak & Yeti

L D **$$–$$$** 🎭

Grab a set of chopsticks and dig in! This elaborate venue is a much-welcome addition to the small Animal Kingdom family of table-service eateries. Nestled deep in the park's village of Anandapur (across from the entrance to the Kali River Rapids attraction), the restaurant—which opens at 10 A.M.—specializes in Asian-fusion cuisine. Reservations are recommended. Its shop offers goods ranging from sushi plates to fine teapots. There is a quick-service area nearby. It serves lunch and dinner.

RiGHT UP OUR ALLEY!

Bowling alleys have never been known for fine cuisine . . . until now. Splitsville invites guests of all ages to take a break between games and nosh on nibbles such as sautéed calamari, blackened mahi mahi, hand-tossed pizzas, made-to-order sundaes, and red velvet cake. There's a full bar, too. Splitsville is in Downtown Disney, West Side, next to DisneyQuest. 🎭

Downtown Disney

This enclave of shopping, dining, and entertainment is comprised of the Marketplace, the West Side, and the area previously known as Pleasure Island (which is undergoing an extensive metamorphosis). Within this region, you'll find eateries such as Wolfgang Puck Café, House of Blues, Ghirardelli Ice Cream and Chocolate Shop, Planet Hollywood, Rainforest Cafe, and T-Rex: A Prehistoric Family Adventure. Overall, Downtown Disney provides a variety of fast food, table service, cheap eats, and super splurges. Downtown Disney is on Walt Disney World property and can be reached by car, resort bus, or ferry (from select WDW resorts). Note that all areas of this entertainment district are gate and admission free.

HOT TIP

Captain Jack's Restaurant has sailed off into the sunset. If you are in need of a casual seafood fix, we highly recommend Stone Crab Lounge, inside Fulton's Crab House (walk-ins only).

🍽️ Bongos Cuban Cafe (West Side)

L D S **$$–$$$** ❤️

Spicing up the Downtown Disney dining repertoire with a menu driven by Cuban and Latin American flavors, this eatery was created, in part, by singer Gloria Estefan. Its slate of traditional and nouvelle Cuban dishes includes black bean soup (our preferred dish), plantains, steak topped with onions, and flan. The atmosphere here is quite lovely (and often lively). Indoors, the mosaic mural and

HOT TIP

DisneyQuest devotees note: The venue's resident Cheesecake Factory Express is no more. However, you can still tame that appetite you built up after hours of gaming without leaving the confines of DisneyQuest. An eatery called FoodQuest has taken over the space formerly occupied by C.F.E. Admission must be paid to enter DisneyQuest before you can eat at the quick-service restaurant. It serves lunch, dinner, and snacks—and participates in the Disney Dining Plan.

outdoor seating wraps around a three-story pineapple, easily our favorite part of this creatively designed restaurant. A take-out window provides snacks on the go. Diners are sometimes treated to live music (feel free to sway in your seat). A small shop sells items such as shirts and hats emblazoned with the Bongos logo. Reservations are available by calling 407-828-0999.

Earl of Sandwich (Marketplace)

B L D S **$–$$**

This tip-top counter-service establishment is brimming with sweet and savory possibilities. Among the fare standing by is a variety of hot and cold sandwiches (freshly prepared on warm bread), wraps, tossed salads, and homemade desserts. A few more exotic selections, such as Hawaiian BBQ (ham with fresh pineapple and Swiss cheese), The Original 1762 (warm roast beef sandwich with creamy horseradish sauce and cheddar cheese), and Caribbean Jerk Chicken are served, too. The Veggie sandwich is also an option.

Breakfast items include sandwiches and baked goods. There are "grab and go" selections as well. Dessert can be cupcakes, fresh-baked cookies, muffin crowns, or English trifle. Beer, wine, and Kona coffee are on the menu, too. Ample seating is available inside the Earl of Sandwich eatery and at outdoor tables. It is not uncommon to see a very long line here, but it moves rather quickly. The Earl welcomes visitors daily from 8:30 A.M. until 11 P.M.

Fulton's Crab House (Marketplace)

L D S $$$–$$$$ ❤

This regal restaurant, originally known as the *Empress Lilly* (after Walt Disney's wife, Lillian Disney), occupies a three-deck riverboat. Though it looks as if it might set sail at any moment, the replica ship is permanently docked at the edge of Village Lake (near Portobello). Guests board the ship via gangway and are enveloped by polished woods, brass detailing, and nautical nostalgia.

The extensive (albeit pricey) dinner menu changes with the day's arrivals. It's not unusual for Alaskan wild halibut to be seen next to Panama City (Florida) snapper. Signature seafood dishes include Dungeness crab legs; a San Francisco–style seafood stew with king crab, shrimp, scallops, mussels, and fish in a tomato broth; and crab and lobster platters. For landlubbers, bone-in rib-eye, filet mignon, and free-range chicken are all satisfying choices.

For a quicker fix, visit our top choice here: the ravishing raw bar at the adjoining Stone Crab lounge. In fact, for a relatively reasonably priced lunch, it's lounge or bust. If the weather's pleasant, try for a table outside, on the bow of the ship. Reservations are recommended for the restaurant.

🏃 Ghirardelli Ice Cream & Chocolate Shop (Marketplace)

S **$-$$**

What is it about an old-fashioned ice cream parlor that makes just about everybody giddy? Oh, yes, the ice cream. This spot does it one better and throws in its famous chocolate, to boot. Stop in for a chocolatey treat, root beer float, or a malt. Tables are available on a first-come, first-served basis. There is a walk-up counter, too. We often duck in here for a quick cup of coffee and a chocolate chaser. And there's always the potential for a free candy sample. How sweet is that?!

🍽 House of Blues (West Side)

L D S **$$-$$$** ❦

Thanks to the combination of its diverse menu and rustic, folk-art-studded design, House of Blues doesn't disappoint. Favorites include flatbreads (grilled then finished in the pizza oven), lobster mac and cheese, tacos, corn bread, and jambalaya. At the far west of the West Side, H.O.B. is a good choice for a satisfying meal or a late-night bite. Live music is presented in the restaurant and on the front porch on select days. There is a lively gospel brunch every Sunday. Reservations are recommended. To book a table at the House of Blues, call 407-934-BLUE (934-2583).

🍽 Paradiso 37 (between West Side and Marketplace)

L D **$$-$$$** ❦

This dynamic waterfront eatery specializes in "mangled margaritas," stocks 37 kinds of tequila, and boasts the "coldest beer in the world." Oh, and they serve food, too!

Paradiso 37's menu focuses on "street foods" of the Americas (all three of them). Appetizer selections include the signature fire-roasted corn on the cob with a mild pepper sauce and cheese, mac and cheese bites, and potato pancakes. Entrées range from Argentinian skirt steak with chimichurri sauce to Chilean-style salmon and prickly pear shrimp salad. No reservations necessary.

🍴 Planet Hollywood (West Side)

L D S **$$–$$$** 🐭

Chances are, you'll have no trouble finding this restaurant—just keep your eyes peeled for the giant globe. Built on three levels, this colossal sphere is jam-packed with classic movie and television memorabilia. The menu features salads, sandwiches, pasta dishes, burgers, appetizers, fajitas, and dessert specialties. Consider sampling the chicken crunch appetizer, Asian chicken salad, shrimp and bacon club sandwich, or lasagna. Bananas Foster is among the dessert choices. Reservations are recommended.

🍴 Portobello (Marketplace)

L D **$$$** 🐭

This Italian trattoria is drenched in warm colors that match the rustic Italian cuisine. The best seats are on the waterfront porch, and the wood-burning-oven pizzas are still a top choice. Traditional Italian cuisine includes mix-and-match antipasti, hand-crafted sausage, pastas, and fish.

At lunchtime, the menu includes Porto-bello's signature sandwiches, like the pesto-marinated chicken with fontina cheese. For dinner, try the Ravioli Gigante (filled with ricotta and spinach) with tomato, basil, and toasted garlic. The full-service bar offers a solid wine list of Italian favorites, specialty cocktails, and beer. For dessert, it's tough to resist the tiramisu.

🍽️ Raglan Road Irish Pub (between Marketplace and West Side)

`L D S` $$-$$$ 🦦

A wee bit of the Emerald Isle can be found at Disney. The convivial spot features furnishings crafted in Ireland, live music, and a menu with cuisine courtesy of Chef Kevin Dundon, one of Ireland's best-known culinary wizards. Think traditional Irish fare with a modern flair. Instead of plain old fish with your chips, expect lightly sautéed lemon sole. This is one of our favorite places to visit in Downtown Disney. There is no charge to enter here—be it for food or drink.

🍽️ Rainforest Cafe (Marketplace)

`L D S` $$-$$$ 🦦

Lush (and loud) as a jungle, this place is thick with tropical vegetation and fish-filled aquariums (not to mention the occasional thunderstorm). A talking tree offers a stream of ecological insights, and animal experts may be on hand to field questions. Dishes have names like Mogambo (pasta with shrimp), Plant Sandwich (veggies), and Mojo Bones (barbecued ribs). Appetizers and desserts can be shared. Reservations may be made by calling the restaurant: 407-827-8500. Without them, expect quite a wait. Note that there is another Rainforest Cafe at Disney's Animal Kingdom. The A.K. location accepts reservations through 407-WDW-DINE. (Park admission is not required to enter the restaurant, but parking fees apply.)

🍽 T-Rex: A Prehistoric Family Adventure (Marketplace)
L D **$$–$$$** ☙

Dinosaurs throw one heck of a dinner party. See for yourself at this eye-popping dino-themed, interactive feasting facility. When you enter, you'll be greeted by hosts we were all led to believe were extinct. Okay, they're life-size *mechanical* dinosaurs, but they're still pretty cool. As are the waterfalls, bubbling geysers, and fossil dig site. It's all so distracting, you may forget why you came here in the first place. When your stomach starts growling, plan to appease it with anything from Jurassic Salad to Prehistoric Pot Pie. With soup, sandwiches, pasta, seafood, and steaks, this place aims to please everyone. You'll find it near Fulton's Crab House at Downtown Disney Marketplace.

🏃 Wetzel's Pretzels (Marketplace and West Side)
S **$** ☙

Salted or unsalted, buttery or plain—Wetzel's can satisfy most pretzel cravings. Among the choices are the Jalapeño Cheese Melt, the Sinful Cinnamon, and the Three-Cheese varieties. They sell ice cream, too.

🍽 Wolfgang Puck Café (West Side)
L D S **$$$** ☙

One of four Walt Disney World establishments that bear the name Wolfgang Puck, this one offers some of the chef's best-known specialties. Among the spotlighted dishes are pizzas, Thai chicken satay, pasta with fresh vegetables, Chinois chicken salad, and rotisserie chicken. The menu is equal parts sophisticated and straightforward—and very fresh. Plan ahead and save room for dessert. The place is a bit noisy and showing signs of age, but still has its fans.

Sushi lovers take note: Housed within this space is a sushi bar that's as aesthetically appealing as it is palate-pleasing. You can order sushi at the bar and in the café. Reservations are recommended for the café.

Wolfgang Puck Café— The Dining Room (West Side)

D $$$-$$$$

Don't be confused by the name. The Dining Room refers to a separate restaurant that just happens to be in the same building as Wolfgang Puck Café and Express. (We think of it as "Puck's Deluxe.") The formal upstairs Dining Room is devoted to more of Wolfgang Puck's cuisine—for example, Chinois rack of lamb with a spicy cilantro-mint sauce and garlic mashed potatoes. Reservations are recommended.

Wolfgang Puck Express (Marketplace and West Side)

L D S $-$$

Wolfgang Puck turns his talents to fast service and signature treats. Among them are (delicious) wood-fired pizzas, rotisserie chicken, soups, sandwiches, sushi (with regular and low-sodium soy sauce), grown-up-friendly mac and cheese, and salads—including his famous Chinois chicken salad. (The West Side location is tucked inside the Wolfgang Puck Café building, while the Marketplace spot is near the Disney's Days of Christmas shop.)

ATTENTION, COFFEE SNOBS

Face it. For many of us, the magic doesn't start until that first sip of coffee makes its way past our lips. And not just any coffee will do. It must be a half-caf vanilla latte with extra foam! In other words, we have great expectations. Well, we have great news: The standard cup has vastly improved since Disney announced a new partnership with Joffrey's Coffee. Hooray! And that coffee superstar known as Starbucks has also eased its way onto the Disney scene. (There's one located in each theme park.) Select restaurants serve special coffee blends, too. Among our favorite spots to grab a cuppa joe:

- American Adventure (Epcot's World Showcase, a stand near the pavilion)
- Artist Point (Wilderness Lodge)
- Big River Grille & Brewing Works (BoardWalk resort)
- California Grill (Contemporary resort)
- Contemporary resort (lobby coffee bar)
- Flying Fish Cafe (BoardWalk resort)
- 40 Thirst Street (Downtown Disney Marketplace and West Side)
- Fountain View (Epcot's Future World)
- Fresh—Mediterranean Market (Dolphin resort)
- Garden Grove (Swan resort)
- Jiko—The Cooking Place (Animal Kingdom Lodge)
- Kona Cafe (Polynesian resort)
- Kouzzina by Cat Cora (BoardWalk resort)
- Main Street Bakery (Magic Kingdom)
- Picabu (Dolphin resort)

WDW Resots

Each of the nearly 30 resorts at Walt Disney World offers its own set of specially themed eateries. There are clambakes at the Beach Club, luaus at the Polynesian, wild game at the Wilderness Lodge, and beignets at Port Orleans French Quarter. Meals may be served buffet, family, or traditional table-service or fast-food style. Disney characters are often on hand (especially for breakfast), and some snack spots stay open 'round the clock. In fact, the resort dining scene has expanded and been upgraded so much of late that the (occasionally arduous) task of resort-hopping is a more worthwhile experience than ever before.

ALL-STAR RESORTS

 Food Courts

B L D S **$–$$** ❦

Each of the All-Star resorts features a themed central food court. **All-Star Sports** has **End-Zone** food court in **Stadium Hall**. At **All-Star Music**, it's **Intermission** food court in **Melody Hall**. And at the All-Star Movies resort, it is the **World Premiere** food court in **Cinema Hall**. The food courts offer similar food stands—although Movies is a cut above. (It's a bit bigger, brighter, and more modern.) The selections include pasta, pizza, burgers, hot dogs, sandwiches, salads, snacks, and a wide variety of breakfast and baked goods, plus a selection of "grab and go" items. Expect to find lots of kid-pleasers.

ANIMAL KINGDOM LODGE

Boma—Flavors of Africa

B D **$$–$$$** ❦

Designed to resemble an African market-place, Boma offers an impressively diverse selection—the fare served represents the 53 countries that make up Africa. Though the eatery may be described as "cafeteria style," this is not a negative. It's one big buffet with multiple stations, and the food is as good as what you'd expect in a fine dining place.

The all-you-can-eat affair provides an excellent bang for your Disney dining buck. Menu selections include wood-roasted meats and seafood, plus African-inspired soups, a decidedly different watermelon rind salad, and vegetarian offerings. Be sure to leave room for the decadent pastry known as the Amarula Zebra Dome. It's tempting to overeat at a bounteous feast such as this, so consider taking tiny portions of everything. You can go back for seconds of your favorites. The wine list includes selections from various African vineyards. Even if you're not staying at the Lodge, it's worth the trip. Reservations are recommended.

🍽 Jiko—The Cooking Place
D **$$$–$$$$** 🐭

Here at one of the most unusual Walt Disney World dining experiences, Jiko's cuisine is inspired by the tastes of Africa, with influences from around the globe. Start with one of the paper-thin flatbreads (like African-spiced fire-roasted chicken with four cheeses and bacon), grilled wild boar tenderloin, artisan cheeses, or seasonal salads. Kenyan-coffee-rubbed fish is a signature dish, and you may find grilled shrimp curry, braised beef short ribs, seared duck breast, and oak-grilled filet mignon on the menu, too. End your meal with a fabulous cheese course, and/or sweets such as coconut bread pudding or a Tanzanian chocolate and Kenyan coffee mousse.

The impressive wine list is exclusively South African, one of the most extensive collections in the U.S. This is an excellent choice for a grown-up splurge. Though it's hardly a kid favorite (the international, sometimes exotic, cuisine may not appeal to timid palates), there are child-friendly options on the kids' menu. Reservations are recommended. Incidentally, the word *jiko* is Swahili for "the cooking place." The small lounge area offers the full menu, too.

The Mara

B L D S | $–$$ | 🐭

This place has a couple of stations at which hot entrée selections are prepared. There's a "grab and go" department, too. Among the pre-packaged options are sandwiches, salads, fruit, and baked goods.

Sanaa

L D | $$–$$$ | 🐭

Pronounced *sah-NAH*, the name of this eatery means "artwork" in Swahili. The Kidani Village spot has a family-friendly menu featuring Disney's take on African-Indian cuisine. Signature dishes include chicken or shrimp curry and beef short ribs slow-cooked in tandoor ovens. For lunch, try the salad sampler. Even the burgers have an Indian touch, wrapped in soft, warm *naan* (a round flatbread). The breads with chutneys, pickles, and raita (yogurt dip) are superb. Desserts introduce many tastes, from no-sugar-added mango pudding to cardamom butter cake. Reservations are recommended. The quality of the fare here is nothing short of outstanding.

ART OF ANIMATION

Landscape of Flavors

B L D S | $–$$ | 🐭

"Better-for-you" options is the theme of this vividly adorned food court, where everything is made fresh as it is ordered. Four mini shops offer soups, salads, pizza, sandwiches, fresh fruit smoothies, organic teas, beer (including gluten-free), wine, coffee, and juices. Pizzas may be delivered to guestrooms in the resort.

BOARDWALK

Big River Grille & Brewing Works

`L D S` $$–$$$ ❤

A standout for its fresh-brewed ales alone, this unassuming place delivers huge portions of pub grub. The straightforward-but-satisfying menu generally includes burgers and steaks. Sandwiches are a cut above. This restaurant tends to be more low-key than other BoardWalk eateries and makes for a peaceful retreat during the day. The interior has a nice, pubby feel. We like to sit at outdoor tables on the boardwalk. Seating is available on a first-come, first-served basis.

BoardWalk Bakery

`B L D S` $ ❤

On any given morning, there are lines out the door of this bakeshop next door to Kouzzina by Cat Cora. (If you're staying at the BoardWalk resort, this is one of the places to get your morning java jolt.) The menu of fresh-baked goods includes muffins, croissants, and cookies. They have sandwiches and salads, too.

ESPN Club

`L D S` $$–$$$ ❤

For sports fans, this joint is nothing less than a miracle. The spacious, welcoming, occasionally frenzied bar/family restaurant is a hard-core sports club. If there's a game being played, chances are it's on one of the million (okay, hundred—but it feels like a lot more) TVs. If not, a simple request to the bartender may result in a channel change.

The fare includes burgers, wings, grilled fish, sandwiches, and a variety of salads and other entrées. Both the dining room and the bar area serve the full menu. Note that this establishment does not accept reservations. If you want to get a good seat, get there long before game time.

📯 Flying Fish Cafe
D $$$-$$$$ 🐾

Fun, sophisticated decor elevates the appeal of this upscale dining destination. In fact, this restaurant could give most fine, big-city gourmet spots a run for their money. (Expect the tab to rival cosmopolitan hot spots, too.)

Chef Tim Keating is a wonderfully inventive chef, and his menu changes often. But you'll always find the signature potato-wrapped snapper with a creamy leek fondue and red wine and butter sauce, the crisp crab cakes, and a char-crusted New York strip steak. We are routinely impressed by the service and find the menu worthy of the price tag. Reservations are highly recommended. Diners without reservations may sit at the counter (we like to sit by the open flames of the grill [shielded by the safety glass, of course]—we enjoy the show). As far as the Disney Dining Plan goes, this is a "Signature" restaurant.

📯 Kouzzina by Cat Cora
B D $$-$$$ 🐾

This eatery on the BoardWalk block comes courtesy of celebrity chef Cat Cora (of *Iron Chef* fame). Mediterranean-style cuisine is the name of the game here. Breakfast includes Kouzzina's signature blend of press-pot coffee, and a delectable icy Greek frappé. In addition to Greek-style yogurt with fresh fruit

and house-made granola, morning offerings
include turkey-sweet potato hash with eggs
and arugula salad; and spinach-tomato-feta
scrambled eggs. Dinner starters include crisp
calamari, goat-cheese-stuffed grape leaves,
spinach pie, and Greek salad. The main
course menu offers cinnamon stewed chicken,
wood-grilled rib-eye steak, and traditional
whole fish. Consider such accompaniments
as garlic-rosemary potatoes, sautéed brussels
sprouts with capers and lemon, and herbed
orzo with olive oil and cheese. Kids' selections
include grilled fish and grilled chicken strips.
Traditional baklava and dense, rich chocolate
budino (pudding) are dessert favorites.
Reservations are recommended.

✈ Seashore Sweets'
S $

A cheery, old-fashioned sweetshop, this spot
sells housemade candies, saltwater taffy,
housemade ice cream, sorbet, and frozen
yogurt. It's next door to the Flying Fish Cafe.

CARIBBEAN BEACH

✈ Old Port Royale Food Court
B L D S $–$$ 🐭

A cluster of side-by-side, walk-up windows,
this basic food court caters to families.
Market Street Grab 'N Go serves croissants,
rolls, pastries, and other fresh-baked treats.
Soups, salads, and hot and cold sandwiches
make up the selections at **Montego's
Deli**. Burgers and chicken sandwiches are
among the many offerings at **Port Royale
Hamburger Shop**. In addition to pizza, the
Royale Pizza & Pasta Shop serves Italian

specialties. **Bridgetown Broiler Shop** serves made-to-order omelets for breakfast and a selection of dinner items, such as carved turkey and pork loin.

🍽 Shutters at Old Port Royale
`D` `S` `$$–$$$` 🐭

The dining room here is as kid-friendly as a table-service eatery can be. Some of the spruced-up menu highlights include chorizo-black bean soup, fresh fish with yucca dumplings and curry-lemon butter sauce, and char-crusted New York strip steak with mashed sweet potatoes. The eatery is in the Old Port Royale building, across from the food court. In addition to soft drinks, beer, wine, and cocktails are served. Reservations are recommended.

CONTEMPORARY

🍽 California Grill
`D` `$$$–$$$$` 🐭

Delighting diners for decades, the World famous California Grill boasts a bold new look and tantalizingly tweaked menu. The West Coast theme shines through in dishes prepared with the freshest seasonal and local produce available. The wine list—which is updated daily—is a mix of greatest hits and good finds. (At press time, several vintages were available by the glass.) Also drawing a happy crowd: the Grill's sumptuous sushi bar, and a host of vegetarian choices. House-made desserts provide the finishing touches, and there are sweeping views of the Magic Kingdom (from select seats).

The restaurant is consistently crowded and the food is first-rate. Reservations are necessary and must be booked with a credit card. Changes or cancellations must be made at least 24 hours ahead to avoid the $10 per person fee. This is a Disney Dining Plan "Signature" restaurant (so it requires two table-service credits per diner).

An outdoor perch (exclusively available to California Grill patrons) affords bird's-eye views of the Magic Kingdom. Guests (including those planning to visit the lounge) check in on the hotel's second floor and are escorted to the restaurant's express elevator. Doors open at 5 P.M. Specifics may change in 2014.

🍽️ Chef Mickey's
B D **$$–$$$** 🐭

Sprawling across the cavernous fourth floor of the Contemporary is one of the biggest kid-pleasers at Walt Disney World. Here, Chef Mickey and his friends host a very popular buffet feast. The changing menu takes advantage of seasonal offerings; a sundae bar provides a sweet finish.

STOCK THAT FRiDGE

Hotel rooms in all Walt Disney resorts come with mini refrigerators—yes, now even the Value resorts have fridges (at no extra charge to guests). The fridges are handy for milk and baby products, snacks, and small amounts of groceries.

If you'd like to have groceries delivered to your Walt Disney World resort, consider www.gardengrocer.com. We appreciate their selection and reliable service. **Note:** Garden Grocer is in no way affiliated with the Walt Disney Company.

At some point during the meal, Chef Mickey will stop by your table, as will several of his friends. Be prepared to drop your fork and swing your napkin with Mickey on a moment's notice. Kids adore this place. Reservations are a must.

Contempo Café

B L D S $–$$

If you head to the first floor in search of the snack bar that's been there since 1971, you're in for a surprise: It moved! All the way to the fourth floor. Peruse the menu on electronic boards with color photos, place your order, then head to the cashier. A pager blinks when food is ready for pick-up. (It's confusing for first-timers. Don't be shy about asking for guidance.) Thin-crust pizzas, sandwiches, and soups are among the selections. A "grab and go" section has drinks, salads, and fresh fruit.

The Wave . . . of American Flavors

B L D $$–$$$

Casual and fun, The Wave brings a surge of dining ideas to Disney. Starting with organic Colombian coffee served with the bountiful buffet breakfast, you know this is going to be different. At lunch, seasonal soups, oversize salads, and a vegetarian sandwich vie for attention with a classic Reuben and a bison burger. At dinner, we highly recommend a lump crab cake starter, followed with the sustainable fish of the day or the locally sourced all-natural pork tenderloin. You can end on a sweet note with tempting desserts that include no-sugar-added options.

The wine program, with mostly screw-cap wines, focuses on bright-style New World wines (an impressive 50 choices are available by the glass). Beer fans get several craft beer selections available in flight samplers. Reservations are recommended. The cool adjacent lounge is perfect for an aperitif or after-dinner drink.

CORONADO SPRINGS

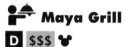 Maya Grill
D **$$$** 🍴

Guests here dine inside a Mayan pyramid, beside a volcano (dormant, of course). The menu has a bit of everything: seafood, meat, and poultry, with a touch of Latino spices added to some of the creations. The pulled-pork empanada and grilled calamari are interesting starts to dinner. Entrées range from grilled sirloin or pork chop to pan-seared salmon, with many dishes cooked over an open-pit wood-fire grill. Desserts include spiced churros and chocolate cake. Dinner is usually served from 6 P.M. until 9 P.M. Reservations are recommended.

Pepper Market
B L D S **$-$$** 🍴

This busy-but-bedraggled spot has a large seating area and many food stands to choose from. The concept here has been tweaked a bit—instead of wandering the food-court-style stations and paying for individual selections, each meal is a set price and guests dine as if they were at a buffet. The "all you care to eat" selections range from roast beef (or pork or turkey) to paninis, pizza, pasta, salads, and Mexican fare—all prepared from scratch. Non-alcoholic drinks are included, and anything can be ordered "to go." Everything is paid for at meal's end, as guests file past the cashier at the exit. Note that a ten percent gratuity is automatically included when you eat in the dining area (we have no idea why). Given this resort's popularity with the convention set, expect a proliferation of people during weekday breakfast and lunch times. Specifics may change in 2014—at press time a renovation was long overdue.

DINNER AT SEA

For Disney's ultimate dinner-and-a-show splurge, consider reserving the elegant *Grand I* yacht. You and up to 17 lucky invitees can enjoy a private tour of the lakes near the Magic Kingdom capped off with a viewing of Wishes, the park's fireworks show—all the while devouring delightful delicacies prepared by chefs at the Grand Floridian resort. The possibilities range from an intimate cruise for two, complete with dinner and champagne, to a swinging cocktail party for 18, with a boatload of shrimp, chips, wings, beer, and wine.

It costs about $520 (plus tax) per hour to rent the 5-room floating fantasyland. Driver and deckhand are included; refreshments are not. To book, call 407-WDW-PLAY at least 24 hours and up to 90 days ahead. The *Grand I* docks at the Grand Floridian but can pick up passengers at the Contemporary, Polynesian, and Wilderness Lodge.

DISNEY'S OLD KEY WEST

Good's Food to Go
`B L D S` **$** 🔴

A walk-up window with a simple menu: hamburgers, cheeseburgers, grilled chicken sandwiches, salads, ice cream, and breakfast selections are among the offerings.

🍽 Olivia's Cafe
`B L D` **$–$$** 🔴

We thoroughly enjoy the Key West manner with which Olivia's approaches its theme. The laid-back setting and menu convey the spirit of the leisure-centric locale. Breakfast includes standards, but also some interesting combos like poached eggs served over sweet potato hash, topped with Key West hollandaise. The all-day menu for lunch and dinner offers salads, conch chowder, crab cakes, seared scallops, burgers, and sandwiches. End with a Key lime tart, chocolate cake, or a banana bread pudding sundae. The menu changes seasonally. Wine, beer, and specialty cocktails are served. Reservations are recommended.

FORT WILDERNESS

🍽 Trail's End Restaurant
`B L D S` **$–$$** 🔴

True, it's a bit out of the way for anyone but Fort Wilderness guests (and even for some of them!), but for many, this rustic and unassuming spot is well worth the trip.

The informal log-walled restaurant offers a hearty buffet breakfast. The fare is not exactly gourmet, but it is bountiful. Breakfast selections include grits, biscuits, gravy, and a tasty "breakfast pizza." The à la carte lunch offers chicken and pumpkin-waffle sandwiches, pan-seared catfish, and spicy grilled shrimp and sausage. For dinner, expect a buffet of smoked pork ribs, shrimp, fried chicken, carved meats, a salad bar, and several sides and dessert items. Pizza and light items are available from 4 P.M. until 10 P.M. Beer, wine, and soft drinks are served. Reservations are recommended. Breakfast costs about $16 for adults, $10 for kids; lunch is à la carte; dinner is about $23 for adults, $13 for kids. After the meal, guests may chat and relax in rocking chairs on the porch. It's off the beaten path, but for many visitors it's worth the trek—this place is quite the bargain. If you plan to eat here, allow a little extra travel time, just in case.

GRAND FLORIDIAN

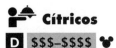 Cítricos

D $$$–$$$$ 🐭

From the aromas wafting from the open kitchen, it's clear that the chef has vowed to wow you with cuisine from the Americas and the Mediterranean, herb by fragrant herb. The fare varies seasonally but may include such items as sautéed shrimp with tomato, lemon, and feta cheese; or braised veal shank. Adventurous palates are most at home here. The menu's not extensive, but the wine list is. There is a private party room for parties of up to 12. Food may be ordered in the lounge, too (ask the bartender for a menu). Reservations are recommended for the restaurant.

ONE LUMP OR TWO?

Teatime with all the à la carte trimmings —scones, tiny sandwiches, and pastries served on bone china—is at 2 P.M. in the Garden View Tea Room at the Grand Floridian. A large selection of teas (some custom blends are made exclusively for this establishment) and tasty accompaniments are offered every day until approximately 4:30 P.M. Reservations are strongly recommended. Call 407-WDW-DINE.

Gasparilla Island Grill
`B L D S` `$–$$` ♥

The mainstays at this recently refreshed 24-hour snack bar are breakfast selections such as scrambled eggs, pancakes, oatmeal, and muffins. Lunch and dinner feature freshly prepared sandwiches, burgers, and flatbreads. There's a create-your-own salad counter, too. Fruit, cereal, packaged snacks, soft drinks, beer, and wine are also available. We prefer to eat outdoors beside the marina, but the expanded indoor seating is nice, too.

Grand Floridian Cafe
`B L D` `$$$` ♥

A pleasant spot any time of day (there's so much old-world atmosphere here, you'd almost expect to see ladies twirling parasols in the midday sun and Scott Joplin playing "The Entertainer" on a grand piano), the cafe is a relatively reasonably priced, low-key way to check out the poshest WDW resort.

The à la carte breakfast extends a wee bit beyond the usual fare. Lunch and dinner menus vary seasonally but they have traditional American dishes: onion soup, burgers, and the signature Grand Floridian sandwich. The wine selection is excellent. Reservations are recommended, but it may be possible to get a table if you're willing to wait. (The restaurant is closed between 11 A.M. and 11:45 A.M.)

Narcoossee's
D $$$–$$$$ ♥

Named for a nearby Central Florida town, Narcoossee's specializes in fresh fish dishes—with the occasional land-based entrée making surf-and-turf combinations a decadent possibility. Narcoossee's menu has upscale selections (and prices), but the atmosphere is casual and, more than occasionally, clamorous. The display kitchen presents dishes such as steamed mussels, grilled steak, and Maine lobster. The international wine selection is quite good—you might even enjoy a pre-dinner glass on the veranda. The view of the Seven Seas Lagoon and the Magic Kingdom (in the distance) completes the experience. Reservations are recommended. The lounge in the restaurant offers a full menu, too (and does not require a reservation). The dress code here is business casual.

1900 Park Fare
B D $$$ ♥

The atmosphere is reminiscent of an old-time amusement park, but the sophisticated buffet menu and subtle decor make this one of the most elegant character restaurants on the property. Mary Poppins and friends (characters vary) mingle with guests during the bountiful daily breakfast. Cinderella and her cronies visit the dining room during the dinner hours.

Keep in mind that the lineup of characters does change from time to time.

Dinner features seafood, salads, pastas, vegetables, breads, carved meats, and house-made desserts. The offerings change weekly, and some may be customized. A salad bar and dessert bar stand nearby. There's a kids' buffet, too. It offers pizza, pasta, and vegetables. The restaurant's focal point is Big Bertha, a band organ built in Paris nearly a century ago. She sits in a proscenium and rises 15 feet above the floor, occasionally bursting into a musical serenade. Reservations are recommended.

🍴 Victoria & Albert's
D **$$$$** 🐭

This elegant dining room has the distinction of being Central Florida's only five-diamond restaurant, an honor awarded by AAA. It is indulgent without being too haute to handle (although the steep prices may curb your enthusiasm) and is considered by many to be the *grande dame* of the Disney dining scene.

The seven-course prix fixe menu changes frequently, always offering a selection of farm-fresh fish, poultry, and beef as main courses. But the beauty of this high-end experience is all the little tastes as you make your way through the $135-per-person (plus gratuity) adventure. You might start with lobster or quail, then move on to seared wild turbot or pork tenderloin. The cheese course is worth every calorie. And, even with seven courses, you must reserve room for the indulgent desserts: a flurry of soufflés, chocolate, and more. Perfect portions keep it all surprisingly manageable. The strains of a harp or violin provide a romantic backdrop. The wine list is encyclopedic. Wine-pairing is available for an additional $65 per person (do let your server know about any personal wine preferences).

At the end of the meal, guests are given a souvenir menu and a red rose (ladies only). In sum, though the experience is an extremely expensive one, for many it is also quite special. Jackets are required for men. Guests must be at least 10 years old to dine here. Reservations are necessary.

For an extra-special (and super splurgy) experience, book the Chef's Table (for up to 10 guests) or the new Queen Victoria Room. With just four tables, the latter provides the restaurant's most exclusive, luxurious setting.

POLYNESIAN

🏃 Capt. Cook's Snack Co.
`B L D S` `$–$$` 🐭

The Captain dispenses snacks and light fare (both prepared and made to order) 24 hours a day. It's a good spot for breakfast items, burgers, flatbreads, Asian noodle bowls, salads, sushi, sandwiches—including the Adult Grilled Cheese (melted cheddar, Swiss, blue cheese, and tomato on multigrain sunflower bread), yogurt, fresh fruit, and snacks. Milk (plain and chocolate), beer, wine, and soft drinks are also available. Come here to buy and fill the Poly's refillable mug with soft drinks. Fans of the Magic Kingdom classic known as Dole Whip, rejoice: the frozen pineapple confection is sold here, too.

🍽 Kona Cafe
`B L D S` `$$–$$$` 🐭

Warm colors, soft lighting, and South Seas decor render the crisp, fluid design of this dining space cozy and casual. The menu

HOTEL PLAZA BLVD. RESORTS

The properties on Hotel Plaza Boulevard—Best Western Lake Buena Vista, Doubletree Guest Suites, Wyndham Lake Buena Vista, Hilton, B in the WDW Resort, Buena Vista Palace, and Holiday Inn at Walt Disney World—sit inside WDW boundaries but are neither owned nor operated by Disney. To make dinner reservations, inquire at the hotel's front desk. Here's the lowdown:

Best Western Lake Buena Vista

Trader's Island Grill serves breakfast and dinner. The **Parakeet Café** offers light breakfast and dinner, plus snacks and to-go items. **Flamingo Cove** serves lunch and cocktails. **Pizza Hut Express** offers pizza (to eat in or take out).

Doubletree Suites by Hilton

Evergreen Cafe offers a breakfast buffet, plus lunch, dinner, sandwiches, and snacks throughout the day. The pool bar is open for lunch and bar snacks seasonally. A market sells snacks and groceries.

Wyndham Lake Buena Vista

LakeView Restaurant serves breakfast and dinner daily; Disney characters come for breakfast on Tuesday, Thursday, and Saturday. **Oasis Bar & Grill** is open for lunch and dinner. **Sundial Cafe 24-7**, a store/snack bar located in the lobby, supplies continental breakfast and light fare around the clock. For drinks, there's the **Eclipse Bar**, **Oasis Bar**, and **Horizons Bar**.

Continued on page 99

tends toward the exotic side as far as Disney restaurants go, but there's a nice variety of choices. Lunch and dinner menus feature Asian-influenced entrées. Possibilities include teriyaki beef, ginger-crusted rib-eye, market-fresh sustainable fish, and barbecued pork chop. The morning meal offers macadamia pineapple pancakes, steak and eggs, and Tonga toast (banana-stuffed, fried sourdough bread coated with cinnamon sugar), plus traditional breakfast items. There is a solid wine list, and island-inspired cocktails are served. The pressed-pot coffee here is among the best you'll find on Disney property. Reservations are recommended.

'Ohana

B D **$$$**

'Ohana delivers a classic Disney experience. It's a meticulously themed, family-friendly restaurant, complete with entertainment. An interesting twist of note: 'Ohana's family-style dinner experience—a South Pacific feast prepared in the restaurant's open-fire cooking pit—does not come with a menu, so no decisions need to be made. The oak-grilled skewers of pork and beef just keep coming. Spicy peel-and-eat shrimp, green salad, pineapple-coconut bread, pan-Asian noodles tossed in peanut sauce, and stir-fried veggies are among the accompaniments, and bread pudding served à la mode with warm caramel sauce is served for dessert. Soft drinks are included. Beer, wine, and cocktails are extra.

'Ohana's setting, which features wood carvings under a vast thatched roof, is rather festive. So much so that there are periodic, boisterous hula hoop, limbo, and coconut-rolling contests for the little ones. Polynesian singers croon from time to time.

Continued from page 97

Buena Vista Palace Hotel & Spa

The new **Avu-Avu Island Grill** offers a family-style, all-you-can-eat Polynesian-inspired menu. The lakeside **Watercress Cafe** serves breakfast and lunch (Minnie and Pluto are in attendance for Sunday breakfast); the **Watercress Mini Market** is open from 6 A.M. to midnight for baked goods, salads, sandwiches, and more; the **Lobby Lounge** provides a place to sip a glass of fine wine; armchair quarterbacks cheer for the **Kook Sports Bar**. **Castaway Grill** and **Shipwreck Bar** serve snacks and drinks.

Hilton

Andiamo Italian Bistro & Grille offers American and Italian fare, while **Benihana Steakhouse & Sushi** serves Japanese favorites. Both serve dinner only. **Covington Mill** serves breakfast (with Disney characters in attendance on Sunday) and lunch only. **Rum Largo Poolside Bar & Cafe** offers burgers, sandwiches, salads, and tropical drinks alfresco. **Main Street Market**, open 24 hours, is part deli, part country store.

For light meals, snacks, or drinks, drop by **John T's Lounge**; specialty coffees and ice cream are served at **Mugs**.

Holiday Inn at Walt Disney World

The newly remodeled hotel has several dining options. The **Palm Breezes Restaurant & Bar** offers three meals a

Continued on page 101

Breakfast is also a family affair—make that extended family, as Lilo, Stitch, Mickey, and Pluto host a morning character meal. Breakfast fare is basic and presented family style. (Platters are shared by the whole party.) Reservations are recommended.

POP CENTURY

Everything Pop
B L D S $-$$ 🐭

The selection at this colorful, modern food court has included pasta, pizza, chicken, roast turkey, Asian dishes, seafood, burgers, hot dogs, sandwiches, salads, pizza, breakfast items, a build-your-own burrito station, and baked goods (tie-dyed cheesecake!). Savory sides include hummus, olive tapenade, and black bean salad. Feel free to join the cast members as they dance the Twist at 8 A.M. and the Hustle at 6 P.M.

PORT ORLEANS FRENCH QUARTER

Sassagoula Floatworks & Food Factory
B L D S $-$$ 🐭

A food court with a Mardi Gras theme, this spot offers pizza, pasta, burgers, sandwiches, soups, salads, spit-roasted chicken, barbecued ribs, ice cream, and bakery products. The Big Easy is well represented here; New Orleans–inspired menu items include classic gumbo, Creole burgers, po'boy sandwiches, muffalettas, and jambalaya.

Continued from page 99

day. It has a selection of "grab and go" items, too. **Aqua Luna** is a pleasant, casual poolside spot.

B in the Walt Disney World Resort

Giraffe Café offers three meals a day. Kids ages 10 and under eat breakfast free with a paying adult. **Sips** serves snacks and sandwiches. Subject to change.

PORT ORLEANS RIVERSIDE

Boatwright's Dining Hall

D **$$-$$$** ✔

Southern specialties and American comfort food are the big draw here—think prime rib and jambalaya. Beer, wine, and cocktails are available, as are soft drinks. The restaurant is quite popular, as it's the resort's only table-service eatery, so reservations are encouraged. Walk-up guests are typically admitted when the restaurant opens at 5 P.M.

HOT TIP

Guests staying at Port Orleans French Quarter and Riverside may have pizza delivered to their rooms between 4 P.M. and midnight. Call Sassagoula Pizza Express from your resort room telephone to order whole pies, drinks, and sweet snacks. There is a $15 minimum per order, and the Disney Dining Plan is accepted.

WDW RESORTS

🏃 Riverside Mill

B L D S $-$$ 🐭

This food court disguised as a cotton mill (complete with working waterwheel) boasts half a dozen food counters and a sprawling seating area. Expect to find pizza, pasta, fried and grilled chicken, roast turkey, flank steak, burgers, salads, sandwiches (including New Orleans–style muffalettas), baked goods, ice cream, and other snack selections. They're big on "create your own" here, too. (You can design an omelet, salad, and/or pasta dish.) There's ample seating, so it's usually possible to get a table even during the busiest of times. All items may be packaged "to go."

SARATOGA SPRINGS RESORT & SPA

🏃 Artist's Palette

B L D S $-$$ 🐭

Set in a converted artist's loft within Walt Disney World's sprawling resort, this spot offers breakfast, lunch, and dinner. Among the selections are fresh tossed salads, made-to-order sandwiches, pizza, baked goods, and more. There are some grocery items, as well as "grab and go" selections.

🍽 The Turf Club Bar & Grill

D S $$ 🐭

A restaurant-within-a-lounge with an old-fashioned horse racing theme (and a pool table), this eatery serves pasta, prime rib, grilled meats, sustainable fish, snacks, spirits, and more. Reservations are recommended.

MEALS WiTH CHARACTER(S)

Character meals are the icing on the cake—or, in some cases, the whole cake—for many visitors to Walt's World. As with everything else here, dining with Donald, munching with Mickey, or chatting with Cinderella is the stuff of everlasting memories. Not surprisingly, these events are insanely popular, so be sure to get reservations (see page 10) to avoid disappointment. One other thing to note: The characters scheduled to appear can change at a moment's notice, and if you are expecting Mickey, you may get Minnie or one of their friends. Here's a rundown of the spots that invite you to dine with Disney characters (again, characters and other specifics may be different during your Walt Disney World visit):

Akershus Royal Banquet Hall:
Belle, Jasmine, Snow White, Sleeping Beauty, Mulan, and Ariel (see page 38)

Cape May Cafe:
Goofy, Minnie Mouse, and Donald Duck (see page 111)

Chef Mickey's:
Mickey, Minnie, Goofy, and Donald (see page 87)

Cinderella's Royal Table:
Cinderella and her royal friends (see page 20). Cinderella greets guests in the castle lobby, while her princess friends host meals in the dining room.

Continued on page 104

Continued from page 103

Crystal Palace:
Winnie the Pooh, Tigger, Eeyore, and Piglet (see page 28)

Garden Grill:
Chip and Dale (see page 35). Mickey and Pluto may join the fun.

Garden Grove:
Goofy and Pluto host breakfast here on Saturday and Sunday (see page 105). Timon and Rafiki join them for dinner.

Hollywood & Vine:
Enjoy breakfast and lunch with Disney Junior characters Handy Manny, Special Agent Oso, *Little Einsteins'* June, and Jake the Never Land pirate (see page 56).

Mickey's Backyard Barbecue:
Mickey and his pals appear at this Fort Wilderness dinner show (see page 114).

1900 Park Fare:
Stars like Mary Poppins appear at breakfast. Cinderella and friends (see page 94) are here for dinner. Alice and the Mad Hatter host the Wonderland Tea Party.

'Ohana:
Mickey, Lilo, Stitch, and Pluto (see page 98)

Tusker House:
Donald Duck and friends (see page 67)

SWAN & DOLPHIN

🏊 Cabana Bar & Beach Club

`LS` `$`

Burgers, grilled chicken sandwiches, flat-breads, lump crabmeat salad, fish tacos, and more are offered at this alfresco eatery near the Dolphin's pools. There's a full bar, too.

🍽 The Fountain

`LDS` `$$`

Themed as a sophisticated soda fountain, the Dolphin Fountain is a sleek spot to stop for a meal or a sweet snack. Ice cream is the highlight at The Fountain. Flavors have included dark chocolate, cappuccino, and mint chocolate chip. Burgers, hot dogs, sandwiches, soups, and salads are also available.

🍽 Fresh—Mediterranean Market

`BL` `$$–$$$`

If you need a quick bite but are looking for more than fast food, Fresh may fit the bill. The menu has included sandwiches, soups, Caesar salads, and entrées with fish, chicken, and pasta. (Some find it a tad on the expensive side.) They serve Starbucks coffee, too. You'll find this eatery on the Dolphin resort's first floor, next to The Fountain.

🍽 Garden Grove

`BLDS` `$$–$$$`

This Swan eatery means to transport guests to the peaceful gardens of New York's Central Park—and the 25-foot oak tree is a most

RESORT TO RESORT

If you're staying in one resort and dining in another, you need to plan ahead—even if the resorts are linked by monorail or water taxi. Why? The transportation may be operating before dinner, but if you're out late enough you'll have to get yourself home another way.

The good news is you will never be stranded. Bus transportation runs until about 2 A.M.—but it's not direct. If the theme parks are closed, you'll have to take a bus to Downtown Disney and transfer to a bus to your hotel. If the theme parks are open, you can take a bus to any park and transfer to one that's headed to your resort. Keep in mind that the trip can take up to 90 minutes in either direction. If that thought is unpleasant, do what we sometimes do: splurge on a cab. Taxis should run between $10 and $30, depending on the destination and traffic. If you have more than three people in the party, request a van. Ask at your resort's bell services desk.

realistic touch. The restaurant offers a full breakfast menu (with Disney characters in the house on Saturday and Sunday mornings), and salads, sandwiches, and more for lunch. What's the dinner "special"? It comes with a side of Disney characters! Different nights also bring different fare. At press time, Wednesday and Sunday were featuring barbecue; Saturday, Tuesday, and Thursday offered Mediterranean selections; and Monday and Friday served up seafood. Disney characters are on hand for dinner every night and for breakfast

WDW RESORTS

on Saturday and Sunday. Reservations are recommended. Visit *www.swandolphin.com* for additional information.

Il Mulino New York Trattoria

D **$$$–$$$$**

A swank Swan destination, Il Mulino offers upscale Italian cuisine in a relaxed yet vibrant bistro-like setting. Specializing in *piatti per il tavolo*, or family-style dining, the spot is ideal for groups. The seasonal menu is characterized by blends of seasonal ingredients drawn from the Abruzzi region of Italy. Signature items include *gamberi al mulino* (jumbo shrimp with spicy dipping sauce), *gnocchi bolognese* (potato dumplings with meat sauce), *pollo fra diavolo* (chicken in a spicy red sauce with sausage), and *salmone* (sautéed salmon in garlic and olive oil with wild mushrooms and broccoli rabe). *Mangia!*

All dinners begin with an antipasti tasting, on the house. Enjoy it while perusing the wine list's 250 or so Italian varietals. The children's menu has pizza, pasta, and chicken parmigiana. For reservations, call 407-939-3463 or 407-934-1199; or visit *www.swandolphin.com.*

Kimonos

D S **$$–$$$**

In the mood for sushi with a side of karaoke? You've come to the right place! This Swan lounge is an honest-to-goodness karaoke bar (the only one at Walt Disney World). Some guests come to sing, while others are drawn by the sushi, sashimi, and tempura. This spot opens around dinnertime, serving food and drinks. The singing generally gets started at about 9 P.M. or so. A good time (and meal) is generally had by all.

Picabu

B L D S **$$**

A combination cafeteria and convenience store, this Dolphin destination serves sandwiches, salads, burgers, pizza, and more. The merchandise area offers snacks and sundries. It's a bit pricey, but the fare's a cut above average, too. The house coffee is Starbucks. This eatery (and store) stays open 24/7.

Shula's Steak House

D **$$$$**

Like the original Shula's in Miami, this Dolphin dining spot specializes in generous portions of certified Angus beef, plus soups, salads, chicken and fresh fish dishes. For dessert, there's apple crisp, vanilla cheesecake, molten chocolate lava cake, and more. The upscale eatery pays tribute to the 1972 Miami Dolphins—that was the year coach Don Shula led his team to a perfect NFL season. The prices are steep, but the steaks are definitely first-rate and lovingly prepared. Though the interior celebrates the game of football, this is not a casual sports bar. The dress code is business or resort casual. Reservations are recommended. Don't ask for a kids' menu—there isn't one. FYI: Shula's is a frequent winner of *Wine Spectator*'s Award of Excellence.

Splash Grill & Deli

L S **$**

Just steps from the Swan lap pool, Splash serves sandwiches, pizza, and salads. Soft drinks and cocktails are available, too. An assortment of packaged nibbles is also on hand—including a nice selection of organic and gluten-free snacks. Open seasonally.

🍽 Todd English's bluezoo

D $$$–$$$$

A sophisticated member of the WDW dining scene, the menu at this Dolphin spot features coastal cuisine, incorporating an innovative selection of fresh seafood with both international and New American culinary influences. The raw bar's stocked with juicy (if a little pricey) oysters and middleneck clams. If you prefer your seafood cooked, try the chilled poached jumbo shrimp or chilled Maine lobster tail. A popular starter is the brothy clam chowder with salt-cured bacon and oyster crackers. All of the entrées are tempting: from miso-glazed mero to bluezoo's signature dancing fish (roasted on a rotating spit).

Not in the mood for a selection from the sea? Consider dry-aged beef or pan-roasted chicken breast. If you've got room when the dessert menu arrives, expect to be tempted by sweets such as warm chocolate cake with a liquid ganache center. Reservations are recommended. Note that it's possible to get food service at the bar, a plus for small groups or solo diners. Closing time at the bar tends to vary nightly (depending on just how crowded the place is). It's a good idea to get here on the early side.

WILDERNESS LODGE

🍽 Artist Point

D $$$–$$$$ 🐭

The Pacific Northwest theme of this top-notch if underappreciated restaurant is announced in landscape murals, while tall red-framed windows look out to Bay Lake.

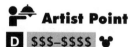

The cavernous dining room is by no means intimate, but it's not without charm.

Artist Point's hallmark is its knack for translating fresh, seasonal ingredients from the Pacific Northwest into flavorful creations. An excellent example is the freshly flown-in salmon served on a smoking cedar plank. The menu may include beef, buffalo, venison, and chicken selections. The wine list features many vintages, including lovely pinot noirs and syrahs from Oregon and Washington State.

For dessert, many loyal visitors swear by the berry cobbler, which is far from the traditional. Ask your server for a description. Reservations are recommended.

Roaring Fork

B L D S $

Set in a stone-walled area (a bit dungeon-like, but in a cool way), this snack bar serves salads, burgers, fries, pizza, sandwiches, chili, and snacks. Breakfast items such as cereal, yogurt, oatmeal, eggs, and french toast are available. Soft drinks, beer, and wine are also offered. This is the spot to top off refillable resort mugs. (Purchase the mug and refill it here for free for the length of your stay.)

Whispering Canyon Cafe

B L D $$$

The name is ironic, as there is nothing quiet about this place. A family favorite, Whispering Canyon is one of the most boisterous Disney restaurants. All meals are offered à la carte and "all you can eat" style. The latter means heaping plates keep coming to the table until you say "when."

Starting at the crack of dawn, the air is filled with aromas of bacon and breakfast potatoes. Lunch offers pulled-pork sandwiches, fish and chips, salads, and more. For supper, expect such items as roast chicken and smoked pork ribs. Reservations are recommended.

YACHT & BEACH CLUB

Beach Club Marketplace
B L D S **$–$$**

The beachy setting extends to this snack bar/ convenience store. There are baked goods, made-to-order sandwiches, and packaged "grab and go" items—small salads, hard-cooked eggs, fruit cups, and more. There is limited seating. If you buy a refillable mug, this is the place to fill 'er up.

Beaches & Cream Soda Shop
L D S **$$**

This classic soda fountain is situated poolside at the Beach Club resort. It serves burgers, griddled pastrami, and chicken Caesar sand-wiches—not to mention ice-cream sundaes, floats, shakes, malts, and sodas. Many of the creamy treats are available to go, too.

Cape May Cafe
B D **$$–$$$**

Goofy and his pals greet Beach Club visitors each morning at this whimsical dining area. The breakfast buffet includes all the standards, plus a few specialties. Breakfast doesn't disappoint, but dinner is the big event here. Dinner is an all-you-can-eat New England–style clambake buffet, and it's one of WDW's most popular meals and better values. The lineup includes crab legs, mussels, steamed clams, carved meats, salads, pastas, corn on the cob, potatoes, and desserts. Soft drinks are included, but cocktails cost extra. It's one of WDW's most popular meals and better values. Reservations are a must.

🍽️ Captain's Grille
B L D **$$–$$$** 🐭

An airy space with a subtle nautical theme, this spot serves steaks and seafood for the whole family. Breakfast offerings include a buffet and a full menu; lunch and dinner are à la carte. Reservations are recommended.

🏃 Hurricane Hanna's Waterside Bar & Grill
L D S **$** 🐭

You can get pulled pork sliders, sea salt fries, seared tuna, burgers, salads, sandwiches, ice cream, and soft drinks at this poolside spot. There is a full bar, too.

🍽️ Yachtsman Steakhouse
D **$$$–$$$$**

You know you're in for a serious steak experience the moment you walk through the door: There's an actual butcher shop here. Yes, the Yachtsman delivers an experience to rival those of revered New York steak houses.

The generous portions begin with house-made dinner rolls and may continue with an appetizer, such as lobster bisque. There's no skimping on the expertly prepared entrées, so good luck finding room for crème brûlée. The menu also includes chicken and seafood. The dining area is pleasant, with several nooks suited for special occasions. It's a great place for a big group enjoy a meal, too. Reservations are recommended.

WDW Dinner Shows

At Disney World, the name of the game is entertainment, so why should dinner be any different? In addition to venues where entertainment comes as a complementary side dish (Biergarten in Epcot, Cosmic Ray's in the Magic Kingdom, Sci-Fi Dine-In Theater in Disney's Hollywood Studios, to name just a few), there are three honest-to-goodness dinner shows to choose from. Given their popularity and longevity (the Hoop-Dee-Doo's been packing houses for nearly four decades), there's plenty of reason to plan ahead and book "dinner as event."

113

Hoop-Dee-Doo Musical Revue (Fort Wilderness) ❤

This family favorite opened in 1974, and it's been going like gangbusters ever since. Every show begins with the stagecoach arrival of a troupe of singers and dancers who proceed to race toward the stage at Fort Wilderness resort's Pioneer Hall. What follows is about 105 minutes of whoopin', hollerin', singing, dancing, and audience participation in a frontier celebration. This being a dinner show, the entertainment comes with unlimited country vittles: ribs, fried chicken (if anything is cold, we request a hot replacement), salad, vegetable, and strawberry shortcake. Soft drinks, wine, and beer are included.

The gags are groaners, but the audience eats 'em up. It's all in the course of an evening at the Hoop-Dee-Doo Musical Revue, presented nightly at 5 P.M., 7:15 P.M., and 9:30 P.M. Cost is about $55 per adult and $28 for children (ages 3 through 9) in Category 3 seating; about $59 for adults and $29 for kids in Category 2; and about $66 for adults and $34 for kids in Category 1. (Category 1 provides the best views of the show.) Prices include tax and gratuity. Reservations are necessary.

The show is presented at Pioneer Hall at Fort Wilderness year-round. Allow yourself plenty of time to get there. The dining room is chilly, especially in the summer. Bring a sweater to combat the air-conditioning.

Mickey's Backyard Barbecue (Fort Wilderness) ❤

It's called a barbecue, but it feels like a country picnic/party, complete with a live band, games for kids, food, and Disney characters.

Presented at an open-air pavilion at Fort Wilderness, the festivities begin with music by a country band. Guests may need a little coaxing to get out on the floor to kick up their heels, and Disney characters join the fun.

Dinner consists of barbecue favorites: ribs, chicken, corn on the cob, and baked beans. Beer, wine, and soft drinks are included.

It goes without saying that kids love it, but it appeals to grown-up tastes as well. In fact, many couples appreciate it as an entertaining and unique Disney night out (somehow, line dancing with Goofy has a universal appeal). For big groups, it's a full-out party. The show is presented seasonally. Call 407-939-3463 for a schedule and to purchase tickets. The cost is about $53 per adult and $31 for kids ages 3 to 9. Prices include tax and gratuity. Reservations are recommended.

HOT TIP

Though outdoors, the Spirit of Aloha and Mickey's Backyard BBQ are sheltered and presented rain or shine—but the former may be canceled if the temperature drops below 50 degrees.

Spirit of Aloha (Polynesian Resort) ❤

A decidedly Disney luau show, the Spirit of Aloha invites guests to participate in a "traditional" island musical celebration. Set in the beachfront backyard of a Hawaiian house (at the Polynesian resort), the experience combines traditional music with more contemporary ditties from the Disney film *Lilo and Stitch*. The show, complete with hula skirts, ukuleles, and fire-knife dancers, takes guests on a whirlwind journey from New Zealand to Samoa. It all stems from a (scripted and hokey) premise about a family member who's moved away and lost touch with her roots. A planned visit from said family member prompts a gathering meant to stir up happy memories of island life.

Presented in an open-air dining theater in Luau Cove, the all-you-can-eat feast is influenced by the flavors of Polynesia. Menu items include roasted chicken, stir-fried rice, and vegetables. The kids' menu features PB&J sandwiches, mac and cheese, and hot dogs. Beer, wine, soft drinks, and dessert are included. Cost is about $59 per adult and $30 for children (ages 3 through 9) in Category 3 seating; $63 for adults and $31 for kids in Category 2; and $70 for adults and $36 for kids in Category 1. (Category 1 provides the best views of the show.) Prices include tax and gratuity and are subject to change. Reservations are necessary.

Plan to arrive about 30 minutes early, and allow extra time for transportation. The show may be canceled due to bad weather.

BOOKING DINNER SHOWS

Dinner shows may be booked up to 180 days ahead by calling 407-WDW-DINE (939-3463). Groups of eight or more should call 407-939-7707.

A credit card number is required for all dinner show reservations. Also, it's very important to remember that cancellations for dinner shows must be made at least 48 hours prior to showtime to avoid paying full price.

To make reservations for Walt Disney World restaurants, dial 407-WDW-DINE (939-3463). The dinner shows are quite popular, so reserve as soon as possible.

WDW Pubs & Lounges

What distinguishes Walt Disney World pubs and lounges from many bars in the real world? Well, in addition to over-the-top theming, you can almost always get a savory nibble to accompany that cocktail. Most WDW lounges serve food, be it from their own menu, or from that of a neighboring restaurant. Hours vary according to venue, but the hot spots at Downtown Disney are usually hopping into the wee hours of the morning.

117

Theme Parks

ANIMAL KINGDOM

WDW PUBS & LOUNGES

Dawa Bar

A thatched roof provides shade, while the sounds of African music (occasionally live) fill the air. A full bar, including Safari Amber beer, is available. It is beside the Tusker House restaurant in Harambe.

Rainforest Cafe

The colorful Magic Mushroom bar serves, among other things, fruit blends and specialty drinks. Bar stools resemble animal legs (hooves and all). The bar is attached to Rainforest Cafe. Admission to the Animal Kingdom is not necessary to enter. It's possible to order off the restaurant's menu from here, too (see page 65).

EPCOT

Rose & Crown Pub ❦

This watering hole—a veritable symphony of polished woods, brass, and etched glass— adjoins the Rose & Crown Dining Room in the United Kingdom pavilion (see page 48). British, Scottish, and Irish beers are available, along with a score of specialty drinks and appetizing snacks imported from the other side of the Atlantic. On special occasions, there may be live (and lively) piano music.

Sommerfest ☻

Just outside the Biergarten restaurant in Germany (see page 39), there's a shaded spot where soft pretzels, bratwurst, frankfurters, Black Forest cake, and German beer and wine are available.

DISNEY'S HOLLYWOOD STUDIOS

Tune-In Lounge

A sitcom living-room setting, with comfy couches and chairs, characterizes this lounge next to the 50's Prime Time Cafe. Waiters play the roles of sitcom moms and dads, and old TV sets play scenes from beloved sitcoms (all of which feature food). A full bar is available. Appetizers and entrées may be ordered from the attached restaurant (see page 54).

NO PROOF NECESSARY

Soft drinks, fruit juices, and specialty drinks sans alcohol are available at all Walt Disney World bars and lounges. Just ask the bartender.

Resorts

ALL-STAR RESORTS

Pool Bars

There are small poolside oases in All-Star Movies, All-Star Music, and All-Star Sports: Silver Screen Spirits, Singing Spirits, and Team Spirits, respectively. Each serves a selection of beer, wine, traditional cocktails, and specialty drinks.

ANIMAL KINGDOM LODGE

Capetown Lounge and Wine Bar

A small lounge area within Jiko—The Cooking Place, this spot offers a selection of African wines and other spirited beverages.

Maji Pool Bar ꙮ

A tiny, poolside spot (in Kidani Village), this bar serves cocktails, soft drinks, and snacks until the sun starts to set.

DID YOU KNOW?

At Epcot's Rose & Crown Pub (located in the United Kingdom pavilion at World Showcase), a specially designed ale warmer can heat your Guinness to 55 degrees—the temperature favored by some authentic British pubs.

Sanaa

Located in the resort's Kidani Village, this lounge is adjacent to the restaurant (see page 82) of the same name. South African beers and wines are the specialties of the house.

Uzima Springs

A poolside bar, this small spot serves drinks and snacks during pool hours.

Victoria Falls

A pretty, mezzanine-level lounge overlooking Boma—Flavors of Africa (see page 80) and a waterfall, this bar serves beer and wine with African influences, plus cocktails.

BOARDWALK

Atlantic Dance

This dance hall showcases music (and videos) from the past and present. There's a full bar and a variety of specialty drinks. Guests must be at least 21 years old with proper ID to enter.

Belle Vue Lounge ❦

Each evening, a full bar accompanies old-time tunes from antique radios in this cozy lounge. Board games are available for on-site use.

Big River Grille & Brewing Works ❦

A working brewpub, this is where patrons may order appetizers at the bar and sample the brewmaster's flagship ales and specialty beers (see page 83).

ESPN Club ❦

The ultimate sports bar provides live broadcasts, along with a menu of ballpark favorites. Occasional trivia contests (with prizes) invite participation by patrons. It's a sports fan's dream come true (see page 83).

Jellyrolls

Dueling pianos and lively sing-alongs are
the draw at this club, serving beer and other
drinks. There is a cover charge of about $10
(but it can vary). The piano players encourage
requests. Don't forget to make the tip jar
happy. Guests must be 21 (with proper ID)
to enter. It's chilly in here—bring a sweater.

Leaping Horse Libations 😈

The poolside bar offers all manner of
cocktails—including frozen ones—plus
sandwiches in a carnival setting.

CARIBBEAN BEACH

Banana Cabana

Refreshing beverages (cocktails and soft
drinks) are served at this poolside bar.

CONTEMPORARY

California Grill Lounge

Prime 15th-story digs afford an eye-level view
of the Magic Kingdom fireworks. A selection
of California wines, as well as other drinks,
plus a full menu, are offered in this tiny space
within the California Grill restaurant (see page
86). The space was completely refurbished and
redesigned in 2013. It opens at 5 P.M. daily.

DID YOU KNOW?

The Contemporary resort's California Grill
serves about 70 pounds of tomatoes *every
night* during tomato season (July through
November).

Outer Rim

This small lounge overlooking Bay Lake serves all manner of cocktails. It's located on the Grand Concourse level of the resort.

Sand Bar 🐭

A full bar is offered poolside, weather permitting. The frozen piña coladas are certainly something to write home about. Fast food in the form of burgers, sandwiches, and salads is available at the adjacent counter area.

The Wave Lounge 🐭

On the first floor of the resort, this spacious bar boasts a wine list that is mostly screw cap (yes, that's a *good* thing)—a quaffable selection of New World wines. About 50 are available by the glass; tasting flights are a great choice for those who wish to sample several selections. Also poured: organic beers, ports, and specialty drinks. It's possible to order from The Wave's outstanding menu (see page 88). Our humble opinion? The Wave is one of the very best Disney World lounges. It's an excellent place for groups to gather.

CORONADO SPRINGS

Rix Lounge 🐭

Located in the resort's main building, this eye- and palate-pleasing lounge serves specialty drinks, beer, wine, and tapas-style appetizers (chorizo flatbread, seafood, and more). Cappuccino is an option. Music may be provided by a deejay or live band.

Siestas 🐭

Swimmers can take time out for burgers, sandwiches, tacos, and cocktails at this spot near the pool in the Dig Site area.

FORT WILDERNESS

Crockett's Tavern

Cocktails, beer, and wine are served in a rustic setting. The tavern is inside the Trail's End Restaurant (in Pioneer Hall). Appetizers may be ordered from Trail's End.

GRAND FLORIDIAN

Garden View

A view of the pool and garden area makes this a pleasant place to meet for a drink or dessert. Traditional afternoon tea is also served daily. Reservations are recommended for tea. The tea experience isn't meant to be rushed—allow time to sip slowly. And come hungry, as you'll be tempted with sandwiches and sweets.

Mizner's

Named after the eccentric architect who defined much of the flavor of southeastern Florida's Gold Coast, this handsome retreat is on the second floor of the main building. Ports, brandies, beer, wine, cocktails, and appetizers are featured. The atmosphere is a bit subdued in the early evening but can be raucous as the hours wear on.

Narcoossee's ❣

This lagoonside bar-within-a-restaurant (see page 94) offers international wines, as well as beer, coffee drinks, and cocktails. It's nice to take a drink to the veranda overlooking the Seven Seas Lagoon.

Pool Bars

Beaches Bar & Grill or the Courtyard Bar are good standbys with beer, frozen drinks, and sandwiches, salads, and snacks.

DISNEY'S OLD KEY WEST

Gurgling Suitcase
This pocket-size lounge on the Turtle Krawl boardwalk serves Key West specialties, along with cocktails, plus beer and wine.

Turtle Shack
Refreshments at this poolside spot include drinks and fast-food selections.

POLYNESIAN

Barefoot Bar
An oasis near the pool, this bar serves beer, frozen drinks, and more. Items of note: frozen strawberry daiquiri and piña colada. (We like 'em mixed, aka the Lava Flow.)

Tambu Lounge
Adjoining 'Ohana restaurant, this small tiki bar offers appetizers and cocktails in a tropical setting. There is a TV showing the game of the moment, but the view out the window is much

GOT I.D.?

The legal drinking age in the state of Florida is 21. However, just being 21 isn't enough to get served—you have to prove it. To do so, present a government-issued photo ID. If your driver's license doesn't have a photo, bring it and an official photo ID (a passport is ideal). Otherwise, you'll have to stick to soft drinks. (Some lounges won't even admit you without ID.)

more compelling. (Is that a volcano?) The lounge serves as a waiting area for 'Ohana and gets busy during dining hours.

POP CENTURY

Petals

An assortment of specialty drinks, as well as beer, wine, and soft drinks, is available at this colorful pool bar.

PORT ORLEANS FRENCH QUARTER

Mardi Grogs

Beer, specialty drinks, soft drinks, and a small selection of snacks are among the offerings at this poolside bar.

Scat Cat's Club

This New Orleans–style jazz lounge offers specialty drinks, appetizers, and occasional entertainment.

PORT ORLEANS RIVERSIDE

Muddy Rivers

The pool bar serves beer, several specialty concoctions, and salty snacks.

River Roost

Designed as a cotton exchange, this lounge features New Orleans specialty draft beers, plus a full bar and light snacks. There's piano-bar-style entertainment Wednesday through Saturday nights, starting at 8:30 P.M.

SWAN & DOLPHIN

Cabana Bar & Beach Club

Beer, frozen drinks, and impressive food selections (crab egg rolls, fish tacos, crab salads, flatbreads, gelato, and more) are the main offerings at this unexpectedly elegant Dolphin poolside spot.

Java Bar

The winding corridors of the Swan lobby have comfortable couches and chairs, punctuated by pianos where musicians often perform. A menu with a variety of specialty coffees and soft drinks is offered daily.

Kimonos

This Swan spot has a full bar and serves sushi and other treats. By night, it's a karaoke/sushi bar. Though big with the convention set, a good time is generally had by all. Come early to get a seat.

Shula's Lounge

This Dolphin watering hole in Shula's Steak House features rich wood tones and comfy seating—the perfect place to sip a cocktail while playing armchair quarterback.

Splash

Beer, frozen drinks, ice cream, and specialty subs are served at this Swan pool bar.

WILDERNESS LODGE

Territory Lounge

Located near Artist Point, this homage to explorers of the Old West is a nice spot for a pre-dinner treat. Appetizers, beer, wine, and specialty drinks are served.

Trout Pass

This Wilderness Lodge poolside bar serves beer, wine, and frozen drinks.

YACHT & BEACH CLUB

Ale and Compass 🐭

The tiny lobby lounge proffers a full bar and has a nice specialty-drink menu (the Bloody Marys are rather special). They're known for their single-malt scotches, too. A light continental breakfast is served daily.

Crew's Cup

Styled after a traditional New England waterfront pub, this inviting lounge has a seafaring feel to it. It's next door to the Yachtsman Steakhouse, and has a nice selection of beer, wine, specialty drinks, teas, and lemonade. There is an appealing appetizer menu, too.

Hurricane Hanna's Waterside Bar & Grill 🐭

This poolside spot, located between the Yacht Club and Beach Club, offers a full bar, as well as light fare and snack items.

Martha's Vineyard

While a full bar is available, wines (by the glass and by the bottle) are the specialties of this house. Appetizers are served.

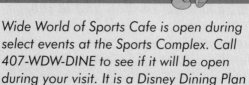

HOT TIP

Wide World of Sports Cafe is open during select events at the Sports Complex. Call 407-WDW-DINE to see if it will be open during your visit. It is a Disney Dining Plan participant.

Downtown Disney

Bongos Cuban Cafe (West Side)

Housed inside a three-story pineapple is one of the more popular cocktail spots at Walt Disney World. There are booths and bar stools. It's possible to order food from the restaurant menu (see page 70).

House of Blues (West Side)

While there is a traditional bar at the back of the restaurant, it's also possible to have drinks in the enclosed Voodoo Garden (table-service only). Guests may order from the restaurant menu (see page 73).

Lava Lounge (Rainforest Cafe, Downtown Disney Marketplace)

This new addition to the recently refurbished Rainforest Cafe serves all manner of cocktails and specialty drinks in a dramatic, volcanic setting. Light fare is served, too.

Raglan Road Irish Pub ❤ (between Marketplace & West Side)

Top o' the evenin' to you! This establishment simply oozes Irish charm. Stop in for a pint and a live music chaser. Guests may sit at tables (and order food) or by the bar. There is no admission charge. *Slainte!* (That's Gaelic for "cheers!")

Shark Bar (T-Rex: A Prehistoric Family Adventure; Marketplace)

Dive into this full-service bar (with an underwater theme) for specialty cocktails such as the T-Rita "cotton-tinis." The bar itself resembles a big wave, and, in lieu of the usual tavern TV, patrons have a colorful aquarium to gaze upon while they imbibe or enjoy a selection from the restaurant's surprisingly good menu (see page 76). Though it's a family establishment (the place features a dinosaur theme, after all), Shark Bar is a grown-ups-only watering hole. You must show proper ID to belly up to the bar.

Splitsville (West Side)

While there's plenty of pizza and beer to keep old-schoolers happy, we appreciate the creative cocktails and novel nibbles at the alfresco area of this bowling behemoth. Select from offerings such as Snickertinis, Kingpin Margaritas, and "Famous Frozen 18-ounce Schooners," plus Tijuana chicken, Juicy Lucy burgers, a selection of sushi, and more.

Stone Crab Lounge (Fulton's Crab House, Marketplace)

Head to the bow of the ship for one of the best scratch Bloody Marys around. They pair quite nicely with the establishment's oyster bar offerings (see page 72). A full selection of beverages (of both the spirited and virgin varieties) is served at a traditional bar and at tables. Reservations are not required, but guests who wish to snag a table should check in at the podium near the entrance.

Wolfgang Puck Café Bar (West Side)

Okay, it's technically a sushi bar (like that's a bad thing...), but this spot is also a great place to grab a stool and relax with an ice-cold beer. There is a TV (expect to see the local game of the moment) and a simple but savory menu—including selections of the aforementioned sushi (see page 76). It's a good choice when caught without a reservation.

WDW Recipes

Your Disney dining experience doesn't have to end when your vacation does. Though sweet souvenirs molded in the image of the Mouse may prove exceptionally satisfying, there may be more substantial culinary cravings to cure. Even if your dining room isn't themed like a drive-in movie theater or a fairy-tale castle, and you rarely entertain princesses or five-foot mice, it's still possible to whip up a little Disney magic in the privacy of your own kitchen. On the pages that follow, we've included some of Walt Disney World's most requested recipes. Just add pixie dust.

Salmon with Leek Fondue

Be Our Guest Restaurant
(Magic Kingdom)

Leek Fondue
½ pound leeks, roots and tough dark green
   tops removed and discarded
½ cup diced white onion
1 teaspoon chili flakes
1 cup orange juice
½ cup white wine
½ teaspoon coarse salt, plus additional
   to taste
2 tablespoons butter
Freshly ground black pepper, to taste

Saffron Potatoes
2 pounds Yukon gold potatoes, quartered
1 teaspoon saffron
1 cup heavy cream
2 tablespoons butter
1 teaspoon coarse salt, plus additional
   to taste
Freshly ground black pepper, to taste

Salmon
4 (7-ounce) skinless salmon fillets
Extra virgin olive oil
Coarse salt and freshly ground black
   pepper, to taste

Garnish
Fresh chives

For leek fondue:
1. Quarter leeks, slice, and place in a bowl of clean water; wash leeks in water, letting any dirt fall to the bottom. Drain and pat dry with paper towels.
2. Combine leeks, onion, and chili flakes in a small saucepan. Add orange juice and wine, stir to combine, and bring to a boil over high heat. Stir in salt.
3. Reduce heat to medium and simmer until leeks are very tender, about 35 minutes. Remove from heat and stir in butter. Season with salt and pepper to taste.

For saffron potatoes:
1. Combine potatoes with enough cold water to cover by 1 inch in a large saucepan. Lightly crush saffron and add to the pan; stir to combine. Bring to a boil over high heat, then simmer, covered, until potatoes are fork-tender, about 10 minutes.
2. Drain potatoes and return to pan over very low heat; add cream and butter, and mash. Season to taste with additional salt and pepper.

For salmon:
1. Season salmon with salt and pepper.
2. Place enough oil in a large sauté pan to lightly coat the bottom. Heat oil over medium-high heat until it shimmers; add salmon fillets and cook until just opaque in the center, approximately 3 to 4 minutes per side, depending on thickness.

To serve:
Place a dollop of saffron potatoes in the center of each serving plate. Place a salmon fillet over potatoes, and top with approximately 3 tablespoons of leek fondue. Garnish with chives, if desired.

Serves 4

Cinnamon Grilled Pork Tenderloin with Cinnamon-Spiced Applesauce

The Wave
(Disney's Contemporary Resort)

Cinnamon Grilled Pork Tenderloin

½ cup olive oil
¾ teaspoon ground cinnamon
¼ teaspoon minced garlic
¼ teaspoon chopped fresh thyme
¼ teaspoon chopped fresh oregano
¼ teaspoon coarse ground salt
¼ teaspoon freshly ground black pepper
24-ounce pork tenderloin, cut into
   4 equal pieces

Cinnamon-Spiced Applesauce

2 Granny Smith apples, peeled, cored,
   and diced
2 tablespoons brown sugar
1 cup apple juice
⅛ teaspoon ground cinnamon
⅛ teaspoon ground nutmeg
⅛ teaspoon ground allspice
1 tablespoon apple cider vinegar

For cinnamon grilled pork tenderloin:

1. Place olive oil, cinnamon, garlic, thyme, oregano, salt, and pepper in a blender and mix on high speed for 5 seconds to combine well.
2. Place pork in a re-sealable plastic bag, and add the marinade. Seal bag and place in a bowl or pan to avoid any leaks. Place in refrigerator for at least 3 hours, or overnight if possible.
3. Remove pork from the bag and discard the marinade. Grill over low heat for 20–25 minutes, or until internal temperature reaches 160°. Turn pork often while grilling.
4. Serve with two tablespoons cinnamon-spiced applesauce on each plate.

For cinnamon-spiced applesauce:

1. Place all ingredients in a heavy-bottomed pot over medium heat, and bring to a simmer. Let cook for 3–5 minutes, or until apples begin to soften.
2. Place the apple mixture in a food processor or blender, and purée until combined.
3. Return the applesauce to the pot, and simmer for another 3–5 minutes, or until the liquid is cooked out.
4. Pour applesauce in a small bowl, cover, and place in the refrigerator until the sauce is completely cooled.

Serves 4

Cook's Note:
If you prefer a thinner applesauce, you may reduce the cooking time in step 3. Cooking it longer not only thickens the sauce, but also concentrates the flavor.

Coriander Chutney

Sanaa
(Disney's Animal Kingdom Lodge)

2 cups cilantro, washed and dried, large
    stems removed
½ cup mint leaves, washed and dried
¼ small jalapeño pepper, seeds and
    stem removed
2 teaspoons peeled minced ginger
2 tablespoons finely chopped yellow onion
Juice from 1 or 2 lemons, depending on the
    size, to taste
1 teaspoon sugar
2 teaspoons coarse salt

Combine all ingredients in a food processor,
and purée until smooth. Refrigerate and use
within 4 to 5 days.

Makes about 1¼ cups

Cook's Note:
This North Indian chutney adds delicious
flavor to any meal. Serve with Indian-style
breads or with grilled meats and seafood.

Naan Bread

Sanaa
(Disney's Animal Kingdom Lodge)

3⅔ cups all-purpose flour
1 tablespoon sugar
1 tablespoon coarse salt
½ tablespoon baking soda
½ cup milk
⅔ cup warm water
1 tablespoon canola oil
4 tablespoons butter, melted

1. Combine flour, sugar, salt, and baking soda in the bowl of an electric mixer fitted with the paddle attachment; stir to combine.
2. Combine milk, water, and oil in a medium bowl; whisk to combine.
3. With the mixer running, pour wet ingredients into dry ingredients. As soon as the mixture comes together, switch attachment to a dough hook, and mix until dough is smooth and no longer sticky. Do not over-mix.
4. Cover bowl with plastic wrap, and set aside at room temperature for 1 hour.
5. Place a pizza stone on a top rack of the oven, positioned approximately 6 inches below the broiler. Preheat oven to 500° for at least 30 minutes.
6. Divide dough evenly into 5 pieces. On a lightly floured surface, roll each piece into an 8-inch circle.
7. Turn oven to broil. Carefully slide one circle of dough onto the preheated pizza stone, and broil until bread is bubbled and golden brown, about 2 to 3 minutes. Watch carefully, as the bread can burn very quickly. Repeat with remaining dough rounds.
8. Brush the warm bread with melted butter, and serve immediately.

Makes 5 (8-inch) breads

Flame Tree BBQ Sauce

Flame Tree Barbecue
(Disney's Animal Kingdom)

1 cup ketchup
¼ cup rice wine vinegar
2 tablespoons molasses
1 tablespoon chili powder
1 tablespoon paprika
1 teaspoon ground turmeric
1 teaspoon ground cumin
½ teaspoon garlic powder
½ teaspoon ground cloves
2 teaspoons onion powder
⅔ cup water
¼ cup packed light brown sugar
1 tablespoon Worcestershire sauce
½ teaspoon salt

Combine all ingredients in a 2-quart saucepan over medium heat. Bring to a simmer, reduce the heat to low, and cook for 25 minutes, stirring frequently.

Use immediately or store in refrigerator for up to two weeks.

Makes 1 cup

Where to Find . . .

From french fries to filet mignon, fried chicken to seared scallops with black truffle spaghettini, Disney dishes truly run the gamut. To help you zero in on the eateries that best fit your needs, we've created a handy index of specialized lists. Once you've settled on a particular spot, flip to its entry in the book to learn more about it. And if there's a category you'd like to see but don't—tell us and we'll try to include it in next year's book.

Bakeries/Pastry Shops
Beach Club Marketplace (Beach Club resort)
BoardWalk Bakery (BoardWalk resort)
Kringla Bakeri og Kafe (Epcot, World Showcase)
Kusafiri Coffee Shop & Bakery (Animal Kingdom, Harambe)
Les Halles Boulangerie Patisserie (Epcot, World Showcase)
Main Street Bakery (Magic Kingdom, Main Street, U.S.A.)
Starring Rolls Cafe (Disney's Hollywood Studios)
Sunshine Seasons (Epcot, The Land)

Barbecue
Flame Tree Barbecue (Animal Kingdom, DinoLand)
Mickey's Backyard Barbecue (see Dinner Shows, page 114)

Best Bang for the Buffet Buck (all-you-can-eat)
Biergarten (Epcot, World Showcase)
Boma—Flavors of Africa (Animal Kingdom Lodge)
Cape May Cafe (Beach Club resort)
Chef Mickey's (Contemporary resort)
Hollywood & Vine (Disney's Hollywood Studios)
1900 Park Fare (Grand Floridian resort)
Trail's End Restaurant (Fort Wilderness resort)
Tusker House (Animal Kingdom, Harambe)

Best with Babies (table-service)
Akershus Royal Banquet Hall (Epcot, World Showcase)
Biergarten (Epcot, World Showcase)
Chef Mickey's (Contemporary resort)
Crystal Palace (Magic Kingdom, Main Street, U.S.A.)
Donald's Safari Breakfast at Tusker House (Animal
    Kingdom, Harambe)
Garden Grill (Epcot, Future World)
Hollywood & Vine (Disney's Hollywood Studios)
'Ohana (Polynesian resort)
Olivia's Cafe (Disney's Old Key West resort)
Rainforest Cafe (Animal Kingdom and Downtown Disney)
Shutters at Old Port Royale (Caribbean Beach resort)
Tony's Town Square (Magic Kingdom, Main Street, U.S.A.)
Trail's End Restaurant (Fort Wilderness resort)

Brunch
House of Blues (Downtown Disney, West Side)

Buffet (all-you-can-eat)
Akershus Royal Banquet Hall (Epcot, World Showcase
  [appetizers only])
Biergarten (Epcot, World Showcase)
Boma—Flavors of Africa (Animal Kingdom Lodge)
Cape May Cafe (Beach Club resort)
Captain's Grille (breakfast only; Yacht Club resort)
Chef Mickey's (Contemporary resort)
Crystal Palace (Magic Kingdom, Main Street, U.S.A.)
Garden Grove (Swan resort)
Hollywood & Vine (Disney's Hollywood Studios)
1900 Park Fare (Grand Floridian resort)
Trail's End Restaurant (breakfast and dinner; Fort Wilderness)
Tusker House (Animal Kingdom, Harambe)
Wave . . . of American Flavors, The (Contemporary resort,
  breakfast only)

Burgers
Backlot Express (Disney's Hollywood Studios)
Cabana Bar & Grill (Dolphin resort)
Capt. Cook's (Polynesian resort)
Cosmic Ray's Starlight Cafe (Magic Kingdom, Tomorrowland)
Electric Umbrella (Epcot, Future World)
ESPN Club (BoardWalk resort)
Everything Pop (Pop Century resort)
Food Courts (All-Star resorts)
Fountain, The (Dolphin resort)
Liberty Inn (Epcot, World Showcase)
Old Port Royale (Caribbean Beach resort)
Pecos Bill Cafe (Magic Kingdom, Frontierland)
Planet Hollywood (Downtown Disney, West Side)
Restaurantosaurus (Animal Kingdom, DinoLand)
Riverside Mill (Port Orleans Riverside resort)
Sassagoula Floatworks & Food Factory (Port Orleans
  French Quarter resort)
Sci-Fi Dine-In Theater (Disney's Hollywood Studios)
Sunset Ranch Market (Disney's Hollywood Studios)

Cheap Eats—Fast Food
Backlot Express (Disney's Hollywood Studios)
Columbia Harbour House (Magic Kingdom, Liberty Square)
Everything Pop! (Pop Century resort)
Flame Tree Barbecue (Animal Kingdom, Discovery Island)
Katsura Grill (Epcot, World Showcase)
Landscape of Flavors (Disney's Art of Animation resort)
Pinocchio Village Haus (Magic Kingdom, Fantasyland)
Pizzafari (Animal Kingdom, Discovery Island)
Restaurantosaurus (Animal Kingdom, DinoLand)
Sommerfest (Epcot, World Showcase)
Starring Rolls Cafe (Disney's Hollywood Studios)
Sunshine Seasons (Epcot, Future World)
Wolfgang Puck Express (Downtown Disney, Marketplace
    and West Side)
Yorkshire County Fish Shop (Epcot, World Showcase)

Cheap Eats (relatively speaking)—Table Service
Beaches & Cream Soda Shop (Beach Club resort)
Cape May Cafe (Beach Club resort)
ESPN Club (BoardWalk resort)
Olivia's Cafe (Disney's Old Key West resort)
Planet Hollywood (Downtown Disney, West Side)
Plaza Restaurant (Magic Kingdom, Main Street, U.S.A.)
Rainforest Cafe (Animal Kingdom and Downtown Disney,
    Marketplace)
Trail's End Restaurant (Fort Wilderness resort)
Tusker House (Animal Kingdom, Harambe)
Via Napoli (Epcot, World Showcase)

Disney Characters (dining with)
(see page 103)

Ethnic Eateries
African
Boma—Flavors of Africa (Animal Kingdom Lodge)
Jiko—The Cooking Place (Animal Kingdom Lodge)
Marrakesh (Epcot, World Showcase)
Sanaa (Animal Kingdom Lodge, Kidani Village)
Tangierine Cafe (Epcot, World Showcase)
Tusker House (Animal Kingdom, Harambe)

American

Artist Point (Wilderness Lodge)
Big River Grille & Brewing Works (BoardWalk resort)
Boatwright's Dining Hall (Port Orleans Riverside resort)
California Grill (Contemporary resort)
ESPN Club (BoardWalk resort)
50's Prime Time Cafe (Disney's Hollywood Studios)
Flying Fish Cafe (BoardWalk resort)
Garden Grill (Epcot, Future World)
Grand Floridian Cafe (Grand Floridian resort)
Hollywood Brown Derby (Disney's Hollywood Studios)
House of Blues (Downtown Disney, West Side)
Liberty Inn (Epcot, World Showcase)
Liberty Tree Tavern (Magic Kingdom, Liberty Square)
Narcoossee's (Grand Floridian resort)
1900 Park Fare (Grand Floridian resort)
Olivia's Cafe (Old Key West resort)
Sci-Fi Dine-In Theater (Disney's Hollywood Studios)
Trail's End Restaurant (Fort Wilderness resort)
Wave . . . of American Flavors, The (Contemporary resort)

British

Earl of Sandwich (Downtown Disney, Marketplace)
Rose & Crown Pub & Dining Room (Epcot, World Showcase)
Yorkshire County Fish Shop (Epcot, World Showcase)

Canadian

Le Cellier Steakhouse (Epcot, World Showcase)

Chinese and Southeast Asian

Lotus Blossom Cafe (Epcot, World Showcase)
Nine Dragons (Epcot, World Showcase)
Yak & Yeti (Animal Kingdom, Asia)

Cuban

Bongos Cuban Cafe (Downtown Disney, West Side)

French

Be Our Guest Restaurant (Magic Kingdom, Fantasyland)
Chefs de France (Epcot, World Showcase)
Les Halles Boulangerie Patisserie (Epcot, World Showcase)
Monsieur Paul (Epcot, World Showcase)

German
Biergarten (Epcot, World Showcase)
Sommerfest (Epcot, World Showcase)

Greek/Mediterranean
Kouzzina by Cat Cora (BoardWalk resort)

Italian/Mediterranean
Il Mulino New York Trattoria (Swan resort)
Mama Melrose's Ristorante Italiano (Disney's
   Hollywood Studios)
Portobello (Downtown Disney, Marketplace)
Tony's Town Square (Magic Kingdom, Main Street, U.S.A.)
Tutto Gusto (Epcot, World Showcase)
Via Napoli (Epcot, World Showcase)

Japanese
Katsura Grill (Epcot, World Showcase)
Kimonos (Swan resort)
Teppan Edo (Epcot, World Showcase)
Tokyo Dining (Epcot, World Showcase)

Mexican/Latin American
La Cantina de San Angel (Epcot, World Showcase)
La Hacienda de San Angel (Epcot, World Showcase)
Maya Grill (Coronado Springs resort)
San Angel Inn (Epcot, World Showcase)
Tortuga Tavern (Magic Kingdom, Adventureland)

Norwegian
Akershus Royal Banquet Hall (Epcot, World Showcase)
Kringla Bakeri og Kafe (Epcot, World Showcase)

Family-style (all-you-can-eat)
Akershus Royal Banquet Hall (Epcot, World Showcase)
Cape May Cafe (Beach Club resort)
Garden Grill (Epcot, Future World)
Garden Grove (Swan resort)
Hoop-Dee-Doo Musical Revue (see page 114)
Liberty Tree Tavern (Magic Kingdom, Liberty Square)
Mickey's Backyard Barbecue (see page 114)
'Ohana (Polynesian resort)

Spirit of Aloha (see page 115)
Whispering Canyon Cafe (Wilderness Lodge)

Fruit
Aloha Isle (Magic Kingdom, Adventureland)
Harambe Fruit Market (Animal Kingdom, Harambe)
Liberty Square Market (Magic Kingdom, Liberty Square)
Sunset Ranch Market (Disney's Hollywood Studios)
Sunshine Seasons (Epcot, Future World)

Good for Groups
Biergarten (Epcot, World Showcase)
Boma—Flavors of Africa (Animal Kingdom Lodge)
California Grill (Contemporary resort)
Cape May Cafe (Beach Club resort)
Crystal Palace (Magic Kingdom, Main Street, U.S.A.)
Flame Tree Barbecue (Animal Kingdom, Discovery Island)
Flying Fish Cafe (BoardWalk resort)
Hollywood & Vine (Disney's Hollywood Studios)
House of Blues (Downtown Disney, West Side)
Kouzzina by Cat Cora (BoardWalk resort)
Mickey's Backyard Barbecue (see page 114)
Mitsukoshi's Teppan Edo (Epcot, World Showcase)
'Ohana (Polynesian resort)
Raglan Road (Downtown Disney, between Marketplace and
    West Side)
Sunshine Seasons (Epcot, Future World)
Todd English's bluezoo (Dolphin resort)
Tusker House (Animal Kingdom, Harambe)
Wave . . . of American Flavors, The (Contemporary resort)
Wolfgang Puck Café (Downtown Disney, West Side)

Hot Dogs
Backlot Express (Disney's Hollywood Studios)
Casey's Corner (Magic Kingdom, Main Street, U.S.A.)
Hurricane Hanna's (Yacht Club resort)
Liberty Inn (Epcot, World Showcase)
Lunching Pad, The (Magic Kingdom, Tomorrowland)
Min and Bill's Dockside Diner (Disney's Hollywood Studios)
Restaurantosaurus (Animal Kingdom, Dinoland)
Sunset Ranch Market (Disney's Hollywood Studios)
Wetzel's Pretzels (Downtown Disney, Marketplace & West Side)

Ice Cream and Frozen Treats

Aloha Isle (Magic Kingdom, Adventureland)
Anandapur Ice Cream Truck (Animal Kingdom, Asia)
Beaches & Cream Soda Shop (Beach Club resort)
Cheshire Cafe (Magic Kingdom, Fantasyland)
Cool Post (Epcot, World Showcase)
Dino-Bite Ice Cream (Animal Kingdom, Dinoland)
Fountain View (Epcot, Future World)
Ghirardelli Ice Cream & Chocolate Shop (Downtown
     Disney, Marketplace)
Hollywood Scoops (Disney's Hollywood Studios)
Min & Bill's Dockside Diner (Disney's Hollywood Studios)
Plaza Ice Cream Parlor (Magic Kingdom, Main Street, U.S.A.)
Plaza Restaurant (Magic Kingdom, Main Street, U.S.A.)
Seashore Sweets' (BoardWalk resort)
Storybook Treats (Magic Kingdom, Fantasyland)
Sunshine Tree Terrace (Magic Kingdom, Adventureland)

Kids' Favorites

Akershus Royal Banquet Hall (Epcot, World Showcase)
Cape May Cafe breakfast (Beach Club resort)
Casey's Corner (Magic Kingdom, Main Street, U.S.A.)
Chef Mickey's (Contemporary resort)
Cinderella's Royal Table (Magic Kingdom, Fantasyland)
Crystal Palace (Magic Kingdom, Main Street, U.S.A.)
50's Prime Time Cafe (Disney's Hollywood Studios)
Garden Grill (Epcot, Future World)
Hoop-Dee-Doo Musical Revue (see page 114)
Liberty Inn (Epcot, World Showcase)
1900 Park Fare (Grand Floridian resort)
'Ohana (Polynesian resort)
Pecos Bill Cafe (Magic Kingdom, Frontierland)
Pinocchio Village Haus (Magic Kingdom, Fantasyland)
Pizzafari (Animal Kingdom, Discovery Island)
Pizza Planet (Disney's Hollywood Studios)
Planet Hollywood (Downtown Disney, West Side)
Rainforest Cafe (Animal Kingdom and Downtown Disney, Marketplace)
Sci-Fi Dine-In Theater (Disney's Hollywood Studios)
Sunset Ranch Market (Disney's Hollywood Studios)
Sunshine Seasons (Epcot, Future World)
Tusker House (Animal Kingdom, Harambe)

T-Rex: A Prehistoric Family Adventure (Downtown Disney, Marketplace)
Whispering Canyon Cafe (Wilderness Lodge)

Knockout Views
Big River Grille & Brewing Works (outdoor seating; BoardWalk)
California Grill (Contemporary resort)
Coral Reef (Epcot, Future World)
La Hacienda de San Angel (Epcot, World Showcase)
Rose & Crown Pub & Dining Room (Epcot, World Showcase)
Sanaa (Animal Kingdom Lodge)
Tomorrowland Terrace (Magic Kingdom, Tomorrowland)

Kosher (fast-food selections)
ABC Commissary (Disney's Hollywood Studios)
Artist's Palette (Saratoga Springs resort)
Cosmic Ray's Starlight Cafe (Magic Kingdom, Tomorrowland)
Everything Pop (Pop Century resort)
Food Courts (All-Star and Port Orleans Riverside resorts)
Gasparilla Island Grill (Grand Floridian resort)
Liberty Inn (Epcot, World Showcase)
Mara, The (Animal Kingdom Lodge)
Old Port Royale (Caribbean Beach resort)
Pizzafari (Animal Kingdom, Discovery Island)
Roaring Fork (Wilderness Lodge)
Sunshine Seasons (Epcot, Future World)

Lounges and Bars (with food)
Big River Grille & Brewing Works (BoardWalk resort)
Cabana Bar & Grill (Dolphin resort)
California Grill Lounge (Contemporary resort)
Cítricos Lounge (Grand Floridian resort)
Crew's Cup (Yacht Club resort)
Crockett's Tavern (Fort Wilderness resort)
ESPN Club (BoardWalk resort)
Garden View (Grand Floridian resort)
Hurricane Hanna's (Yacht & Beach Club resorts)
Il Mulino New York Trattoria Lounge (Swan resort)
Kimonos (Swan resort)
La Cava de Tequila (Epcot, World Showcase)
Leaping Horse Libations (BoardWalk resort)

Mardi Grogs (Port Orleans French Quarter resort)
Martha's Vineyard (Beach Club resort)
Mizner's (Grand Floridian resort)
Muddy Rivers (Port Orleans Riverside resort)
Narcoossee's (Grand Floridian resort)
Outer Rim (Contemporary resort)
Paradiso 37 (Downtown Disney, between Marketplace and West Side)
Portobello (Downtown Disney, Marketplace)
Raglan Road (Downtown Disney, between Marketplace and West Side)
Rainforest Cafe (Magic Mushroom bar; Animal Kingdom and Downtown Disney, Marketplace)
River Roost (Port Orleans Riverside resort)
Rix Lounge (Coronado Springs resort)
Rose & Crown Pub (Epcot, World Showcase)
Sanaa lounge (Animal Kingdom Lodge)
Sand Bar (Contemporary resort)
Siestas (Coronado Springs resort)
Sommerfest (inside Germany; Epcot, World Showcase)
Splash Terrace (Swan resort)
Stone Crab Lounge (inside Fulton's Crab House; Downtown Disney, Marketplace)
Tambu Lounge (Polynesian resort)
Territory Lounge (Wilderness Lodge)
Tune-In Lounge (Disney's Hollywood Studios)
Turf Club Bar & Grill, The (Saratoga Springs resort)
Turtle Shack (Disney's Old Key West resort)
Tutto Gusto (Epcot, World Showcase)
Uzima Springs (Animal Kingdom Lodge)
Yak & Yeti Lounge (Disney's Animal Kingdom)

Open 24 Hours
Capt. Cook's (Polynesian resort)
Gasparilla Island Grill (Grand Floridian resort)
Picabu (Dolphin resort)
Sundial Cafe 24-7 (Wyndham hotel)

Pizza
Capt. Cook's (Polynesian resort)
Everything Pop (Pop Century resort)
Food Courts (All-Star resorts)

Gasparilla Island Grill (Grand Floridian resort)
Mama Melrose's Ristorante Italiano (Disney's Hollywood Studios)
Pinocchio Village Haus (Magic Kingdom, Fantasyland)
Pizza Planet (Disney's Hollywood Studios)
Pizzafari (Animal Kingdom, Discovery Island)
Planet Hollywood (Downtown Disney, West Side)
Riverside Mill (Port Orleans Riverside resort)
Roaring Fork (Wilderness Lodge)
Royale Pizza Shop (Caribbean Beach resort)
Sassagoula Floatworks & Food Factory (Port Orleans
    French Quarter resort)
Sunset Ranch Market (Disney's Hollywood Studios)
Trail's End Restaurant (Fort Wilderness resort)
Via Napoli (Epcot, World Showcase)
Wolfgang Puck Café (Downtown Disney, West Side)
Wolfgang Puck Express (Downtown Disney, Marketplace
    and West Side)

Salads

Artist's Palette (Saratoga Springs resort)
Big River Grille & Brewing Works (BoardWalk resort)
Boma—Flavors of Africa (Animal Kingdom Lodge)
Cape May Cafe (Beach Club resort)
Columbia Harbour House (Magic Kingdom, Liberty Square)
Flame Tree Barbecue (Animal Kingdom, Discovery Island)
Gasparilla Island Grill(Grand Floridian resort)
Hollywood Brown Derby (Disney's Hollywood Studios)
Il Mulino New York Trattoria (Swan resort)
Pecos Bill Cafe (Magic Kingdom, Frontierland)
Pepper Market (Coronado Springs resort)
Pinocchio Village Haus (Magic Kingdom, Fantasyland)
Plaza Restaurant (Magic Kingdom, Main Street, U.S.A.)
Rainforest Cafe (Animal Kingdom and Downtown Disney,
    Marketplace)
Sunshine Seasons (Epcot, Future World)
Wave . . . of American Flavors, The (Contemporary resort)
Wolfgang Puck Café (Downtown Disney, West Side)

Seafood

Artist Point (Wilderness Lodge)
California Grill (Contemporary resort)
Cape May Cafe (Beach Club resort)

Columbia Harbour House (Magic Kingdom, Liberty Square)
Coral Reef (Epcot, Future World)
Flying Fish Cafe (BoardWalk resort)
Fulton's Crab House (Downtown Disney, Marketplace)
Kimonos (Swan resort)
Narcoossee's (Grand Floridian resort)
Todd English's bluezoo (Dolphin resort)
Wave . . . of American Flavors, The (Contemporary resort)

Snack Bars (at the resorts)
Beach Club Marketplace (Beach Club resort)
Cabana Bar & Grill (Dolphin resort)
Capt. Cook's (Polynesian resort)
Contempo Café (Contemporary resort)
Gasparilla Island Grill (Grand Floridian resort)
Mara, The (Animal Kingdom Lodge)
Picabu (Dolphin resort)
Roaring Fork (Wilderness Lodge)
Sand Bar (pool bar; Contemporary resort)

Solo Diners
California Grill (Contemporary resort)
Cítricos lounge (Grand Floridian resort)
Crew's Cup (lounge, Yacht Club resort)
ESPN Club (BoardWalk resort)
Flying Fish Cafe (BoardWalk resort)
Il Mulino New York Trattoria (Swan resort)
Jiko—The Cooking Place lounge (Animal Kingdom Lodge)
Narcoossee's lounge (Grand Floridian resort)
Stone Crab Lounge (inside Fulton's Crab House, Downtown
    Disney, Marketplace)
Tune-In Lounge (Disney's Hollywood Studios)
The Wave . . . of American Flavors Lounge
    (Contemporary resort)
Wolfgang Puck Café Bar (Downtown Disney, West Side)

Steak
Be Our Guest Restaurant (Magic Kingdom, Fantasyland)
Captain's Grille (Yacht Club resort)
La Hacienda de San Angel (Epcot, World Showcase)
Le Cellier Steakhouse (Epcot, World Showcase)
Shula's Steak House (Dolphin resort)

The Wave . . . of American Flavors (Contemporary resort)
Yachtsman Steakhouse (Yacht Club resort)

Super Splurges (for grown-ups)
Artist Point (Wilderness Lodge)
California Grill (Contemporary resort)
Chefs de France (Epcot, World Showcase)
Flying Fish Cafe (BoardWalk resort)
Hollywood Brown Derby (Disney's Hollywood Studios)
Il Mulino (Swan resort)
Jiko—The Cooking Place (Animal Kingdom Lodge)
Le Cellier Steakhouse (Epcot, World Showcase)
Monsieur Paul (Epcot, World Showcase)
Sanaa (Animal Kingdom Lodge)
Shula's Steak House (Dolphin resort)
Victoria & Albert's (Grand Floridian resort)
Yachtsman Steakhouse (Yacht Club resort)

Sushi
California Grill (Contemporary resort)
Capt. Cook's (Polynesian resort)
Katsura Grill (Epcot, World Showcase)
Kimonos (lounge; Swan resort)
Kona Island (after 5 P.M.; Polynesian resort)
Mitsukoshi's Tokyo Dining (Epcot, World Showcase)
Splitsville (Downtown Disney, West Side)
Wolfgang Puck Café (Downtown Disney, West Side)

Terrific Theming
Akershus Royal Banquet Hall (Epcot, World Showcase)
Be Our Guest Restaurant (Magic Kingdom, Fantasyland)
Biergarten (Epcot, World Showcase)
Cinderella's Royal Table (Magic Kingdom, Fantasyland)
50's Prime Time Cafe (Disney's Hollywood Studios)
Liberty Tree Tavern (Magic Kingdom, Liberty Square)
'Ohana (Polynesian resort)
Rainforest Cafe (Animal Kingdom & Downtown Disney, Marketplace)
Sanaa (Animal Kingdom Lodge)
Sci-Fi Dine-In Theater (Disney's Hollywood Studios)
T-Rex: A Prehistoric Family Adventure (Downtown Disney, Marketplace)
Tusker House (Discovery Island, Animal Kingdom)

Vegetarian Selections

Boma—Flavors of Africa (Animal Kingdom Lodge)
Columbia Harbour House (Magic Kingdom, Liberty Square)
Cosmic Ray's Starlight Cafe (Magic Kingdom, Tomorrowland)
Everything Pop (Pop Century resort)
Food Courts (All-Star resorts)
Jiko—The Cooking Place (Animal Kingdom Lodge)
Mama Melrose's Ristorante Italiano (Disney's Hollywood Studios)
Pecos Bill Cafe (Magic Kingdom, Frontierland)
Pizzafari (Animal Kingdom, Discovery Island)
Pinocchio Village Haus (Magic Kingdom, Fantasyland)
Planet Hollywood (Downtown Disney, West Side)
Rainforest Cafe (Animal Kingdom and Downtown Disney, Marketplace)
Sanaa (Animal Kingdom Lodge)
Sunset Ranch Market (Disney's Hollywood Studios)
Sunshine Seasons (Epcot, Future World)
Tony's Town Square (Magic Kingdom, Main Street, U.S.A.)
Tusker House (Animal Kingdom, Harambe)
Wolfgang Puck Express (Downtown Disney, West Side and Marketplace)

Wine and Dine (great wine lists)

Artist Point (Wilderness Lodge)
Be Our Guest Restaurant ([dinner] Magic Kingdom, Fantasyland)
Boma—Flavors of Africa (Animal Kingdom Lodge)
California Grill (Contemporary resort)
Chefs de France (Epcot, World Showcase)
Citricos (Grand Floridian resort)
Flying Fish Cafe (BoardWalk resort)
Hollywood Brown Derby (Disney's Hollywood Studios)
Il Mulino New York Trattoria (Swan resort)
Jiko—The Cooking Place (Animal Kingdom Lodge)
Narcoossee's (Grand Floridian resort)
Portobello (Downtown Disney, Marketplace)
Sanaa (Animal Kingdom Lodge)
Shula's Steak House (Dolphin resort)
Victoria & Albert's (Grand Floridian resort)
Wave . . . of American Flavors, The (Contemporary resort)
Wolfgang Puck Café—The Dining Room (Downtown Disney, West Side)
Yachtsman Steakhouse (Yacht Club resort)

INDEX

INDEX

INDEX

INDEX